Exploring

HEAVENLY PLACES

EQUIPPED FOR HARVEST

VOLUME 13

And he said to them, "The harvest is plentiful, but the laborers are few. Therefore pray earnestly to the Lord of the harvest to send out laborers into his harvest."
Luke 10:2

exploring

HEAVENLY PLACES

EQUIPPED FOR HARVEST

VOLUME 13

BY

Paul L. Cox

Barbara Kain Parker

Brian P. Cox

EXPLORING HEAVENLY PLACES, VOLUME 13
EQUIPPED FOR HARVEST

By:
Paul L. Cox
Barbara Kain Parker
Brian P. Cox

Aslan's Place Publications
9315 Sagebrush Street
Apple Valley, CA 92308
760-810-0990
aslansplace.com

Unless otherwise indicated, scriptures are taken from the: The ESV® Bible (The Holy Bible, English Standard Version®) copyright © 2016 by Crossway Bible, a publishing ministry of Good News Publishers. Used by permission. All rights reserved.

Printed in the United States of America

DEDICATION

We dedicate this book to our dear friend, Jana Green, who went home to be with the Lord on January 26, 2022. Though she is no longer here in body, she remains very much alive and active in spirit, cooperating with the Holy Spirit to do what the Father is doing to establish His kingdom on earth as it is in Heaven.

Jana's life and ministry continue to resonate with all of us who have been fortunate enough to know and love her. We can testify to the truth that Jana was all about seeking greater intimacy with God and equipping others to know and serve the Lord. Whether her name is mentioned or not, many of the prophetic words Jana delivered are included, not only in this volume but also throughout the entire *Exploring Heavenly Places* series. We are forever grateful for her enduring legacy of faith.

Thank you, Jana, for sowing into our lives all that the Father gave you to share. Thank you for your love, your friendship and your prayers. You are sorely missed, but we will see you soon!

TABLE OF CONTENTS

PREFACE

In this volume, we introduce and welcome a new author to the *Exploring Heavenly Places* series. Brian Cox is Paul's son, and he will already be familiar to many of our readers. Brian wears many hats around Aslan's Place, not the least of which often happens behind the scenes. A few of them include:

- Gifted prayer minister and teacher
- Website developer and manager of aslansplace.com
- Producer/editor of the multimedia aspects of the ministry, including both live broadcasts and audio/video recordings
- Coordinator of book production and distribution

Brian has contributed *Chapter Four, Dealing With Offenses Within the Body of Christ.* This is a subject that he often teaches during Aslan's Place academies, and many people have reported back that their lives were changed when they adopted this biblical approach to conflict.

Thank you Brian for all the ways you help build unity within the Body of Christ!

Paul L Cox
Barbara Kain Parker

INTRODUCTION

On September 22, 2009, Jana Green delivered a corporate word to Aslan's Place:

You will overcome.

It has been granted to you to persevere.

Great exploits lay ahead, and you will seize them.

Fear not, a collision of angels is being assigned.

You will seize the opportunity and redeem the time.

The angels of assignment are for opportunity, for alignment and for unity.

You will now know the treasures from the ancient ways that combine the future in these days.

The revelation that has been stored up will now be poured out; it is for so much more, without a doubt.

The wells will spring up, and the rains pour down; both the latter and former will be in the ground.

Evangelism, the like of which has never been seen; signs, wonders and healings will now be received.

It is a star network connected by light; angels on assignment, angels that fight.

Revelation for this age is being released; the treasures of darkness are coming up from the deep.

I am adjusting your vision so you may see the revelation stored up, that you may believe.

Both the harvest and the sower will be in the earth.

IT'S THE ANCIENT OF DAYS!!! (words were shouted)

I AM combining the past of eternity for the future promise.

Hold fast, hold fast until I come.

Pondering what the subtitle should be as I began piecing together the content of this book, the words popped into my mind, *Equipped for Harvest*. I didn't even mention it to Paul or Brian until the manuscript was almost finished because I had no clue how the Lord was going to put it all together and make the subtitle relevant. It wasn't until the final chapter was being written that I finally understood, as I considered using Jana's corporate word there. But the Holy Spirit revealed that it wasn't to be at the end at all, but the beginning.

One might think that since it is a harvest of souls of which we are speaking, the focus of *Equipped for Harvest* would be all about evangelism; but it's not. Instead, it delves into four basic themes that are integral to the God's harvest—unity, grace, sound, and the battle.

Our prayer for this book is that of Hebrews 13:20-22:

> *Now may the God of peace who brought again from the dead our Lord Jesus, the great shepherd of the sheep, by the blood of the eternal covenant, equip you with everything good that you may do his will, working in us that which is pleasing in his sight, through Jesus Christ, to whom be glory forever and ever. Amen.*

Barbara Kain Parker

CHAPTER ONE:
GOOD NEWS, BAD NEWS

Whom among us has been asked, "I've got good news and I've got bad news; which would you like to hear first?" One study revealed that 78% of its respondents wanted to get the bad news out of the way first, with the hope that the good news would offset it and make them feel better.[1] Well folks, we begin this book with just such a scenario, so we might as well go ahead and get the bad news behind us.

The Bible is full of examples of good versus bad, more accurately stated as God's standards of righteousness versus the enemy's evil agenda. It displays the covenant promises and blessings of the Lord right alongside His dire warnings and the terrible consequences when His instructions go unheeded. Therefore, we shouldn't be surprised to see many biblical contrasts between disunity (bad) and unity (good). Bad news first.

Disunity can be defined as disagreement, split, breach, dissent, rupture, alienation, variance, discord, schism, estrangement, dissention and discordance.[2] From Genesis through Revelation, examples abound, with the enemy on the side of all that is evil. God's view is clear that sin is at the root of disunity; it traces back to the Adam's original sin and includes both personal and national sins, all of which result in estrangement from God:

And they heard the sound of the LORD *God walking in the garden in the cool of the day, and the man and his wife hid themselves from the presence of the* LORD *God among the trees of the garden. But the* LORD *God called to the man and said to him, "Where are you?" And he said, "I heard the sound of you in the garden, and I was afraid, because I was naked, and I hid myself." He said, "Who told you that you were naked? Have you eaten of the tree of which I commanded you not to eat?" The man said, The woman whom you gave to be with me, she gave me fruit of the tree, and I ate." Then the* LORD *God said to the woman, "What is this that you have done?" The woman said, "The serpent deceived me, and I ate." [3]*

Hide your face from my sins, and blot out all my iniquities. Create in me a clean heart, O God, and renew a right spirit within me. Cast me not away from your presence, and take not your Holy Spirit from me. Restore to me the joy of your salvation, and uphold me with a willing spirit.[4]

"Is Israel a slave? Is he a homeborn servant? Why then has he become a prey? The lions have roared against him; they have roared loudly. They have made his land a waste; his cities are in ruins, without inhabitant. Moreover, the men of Memphis and Tahpanhes have shaved the crown of your head. Have you not brought this upon yourself by forsaking the LORD your God, when he led you in the way? [5]

The Bible is also clear about those causative sins. To name a few:

Contention: *For lack of wood the fire goes out, and where there is no whisperer, quarreling ceases. As charcoal to hot embers and wood to fire, so is a quarrelsome man for kindling strife. [6]*

Envy: *…for you are still of the flesh. For while there is jealousy and strife among you, are you not of the flesh and behaving only in a human way? [7]*

Lies: *There are six things that the LORD hates, seven that are an abomination to him: haughty eyes, a lying tongue, and hands that shed innocent blood, a heart that devises wicked plans, feet that make haste to run to evil, a false witness who breathes out lies, and one who sows discord among brothers. [8]*

Dishonesty and Violence: *A dishonest man spreads strife, and a whisperer separates close friends. A man of violence entices his neighbor and leads him in a way that is not good. [9]*

Gossip: *Besides that, they learn to be idlers, going about from house to house, and not only idlers, but also gossips and busybodies, saying what they should not.[10]*

Slander: *Whoever goes about slandering reveals secrets, but he who is trustworthy in spirit keeps a thing covered.* [11]

Grumbling: *So the Jews grumbled about him, because he said, "I am the bread that came down from heaven." They said, "Is not this Jesus, the son of Joseph, whose father and mother we know? How does he now say, 'I have come down from heaven'?"* [12]

And the list goes on: *They were filled with all manner of unrighteousness, evil, covetousness, malice. They are full of envy, murder, strife, deceit, maliciousness. They are gossips, slanderers, haters of God, insolent, haughty, boastful, inventors of evil, disobedient to parents, foolish, faithless, heartless, ruthless. Though they know God's righteous decree that those who practice such things deserve to die, they not only do them but give approval to those who practice them.* [13]

Sadly, such disunity is not only a hallmark in the world but also in the Church. In March 2021, the following prophetic word was received:

Many people pray, but there are divisions between the people that do not allow the prayers to join together. Strife, intolerance, religiosity, lawlessness, arrogance and a lot more. Conscious division also comes between; Catholics, Pentecostals, Baptists [and the list goes on]— we stay in our own lane. We do not have the unity that Jesus prayed for, and God is calling us to deal with this division, and then to call them together.

In his short letter, Jude warned *those who are called, beloved in God the Father and kept for Jesus Christ,* [14] of ungodly people who had infiltrated the Church with the intent of sowing discord. Considering the time in which we live, we would be wise to recognize the relevance of his warning:

But you must remember, beloved, the predictions of the apostles of our Lord Jesus Christ. They said to you, "In the last time there will be scoffers, following their own ungodly passions." It is these who cause divisions, worldly people, devoid of the Spirit. [15]

The enemy excels at corrupting everything that is righteous for the purpose of establishing his own evil kingdom. In this familiar account, unity was corrupted but still effective:

> *Now the whole earth had one language and the same words. And as people migrated from the east, they found a plain in the land of Shinar and settled there. And they said to one another, "Come, let us make bricks, and burn them thoroughly." And they had brick for stone, and bitumen for mortar. Then they said, "Come, let us build ourselves a city and a tower with its top in the heavens, and let us make a name for ourselves, lest we be dispersed over the face of the whole earth." And the LORD came down to see the city and the tower, which the children of man had built. And the LORD said, "Behold, they are one people, and they have all one language, and this is only the beginning of what they will do. And nothing that they propose to do will now be impossible for them. Come, let us go down and there confuse their language, so that they may not understand one another's speech." So the LORD dispersed them from there over the face of all the earth, and they left off building the city. Therefore its name was called Babel, because there the LORD confused the language of all the earth. And from there the LORD dispersed them over the face of all the earth.[16]*

The people of Nimrod's kingdom built a tower into the heavens, using ungodly unity to tap into false glory and false unity, using a valid spiritual principle to establish an evil kingdom. The Lord recognized what was happening and, in His wisdom, turned disunity loose among the people by confusing the language. They could no longer communicate and were scattered across the earth.

Ungodly unity always sows seeds of discord; it reared its ugly head time and again throughout the scriptures, as is well illustrated by the persistent agreement of the pharisees against Jesus, the stoning of Stephen, and the persecution of Paul:

> *So the chief priests and the Pharisees gathered the council and said, "What are we to do? For this man performs many signs. If we let him go on like this, everyone will believe in him, and the Romans*

will come and take away both our place and our nation." … So from that day on they made plans to put him to death.[17]

But they cried out with a loud voice and stopped their ears and rushed together at him. Then they cast him out of the city and stoned him. And the witnesses laid down their garments at the feet of a young man named Saul.[18]

But when Gallio was proconsul of Achaia, the Jews made a united attack on Paul and brought him before the tribunal, saying, "This man is persuading people to worship God contrary to the law."[19]

Currently, one need only look at wars and rumors of war, personal and political animosities against anyone who doesn't share one's view, rioting, rampant crime—in other words, the world in general—to observe glaring examples of disunity. Clearly, the enemy is still up to his old tricks thousands of years later, but we can't say we haven't been warned. Jesus himself described in great detail the chaotic world in which we now live.[20]

But enough bad news! Let's turn to the good news, which gives us hope and should definitely make us feel a whole lot better.

Clearly, the enemy is the prime promoter of disunity, so how great it is when God steps in and uses it against him. King David certainly understood this when he wrote:

God shall arise, his enemies shall be scattered; and those who hate him shall flee before him! As smoke is driven away, so you shall drive them away; as wax melts before fire, so the wicked shall perish before God! But the righteous shall be glad; they shall exult before God; they shall be jubilant with joy![21]

This was Gideon's experience, when God whittled his army down to just 300 men who were expected to defeat the forces of Midian, which were innumerable:

That same night the Lord said to him, "Arise, go down against the camp, for I have given it into your hand. But if you are afraid to go down, go down to the camp with Purah your servant. And you shall hear what they say, and afterward your hands shall be strengthened to go down against the camp."... When Gideon came, behold, a man was telling a dream to his comrade. And he said, "Behold, I dreamed a dream, and behold, a cake of barley bread tumbled into the camp of Midian and came to the tent and struck it so that it fell and turned it upside down, so that the tent lay flat." And his comrade answered, "This is no other than the sword of Gideon the son of Joash, a man of Israel; God has given into his hand Midian and all the camp." As soon as Gideon heard the telling of the dream and its interpretation, he worshiped. And he returned to the camp of Israel and said, "Arise, for the Lord has given the host of Midian into your hand."... Then the three companies blew the trumpets and broke the jars. They held in their left hands the torches, and in their right hands the trumpets to blow. And they cried out, "A sword for the Lord and for Gideon!" Every man stood in his place around the camp, and all the army ran. They cried out and fled. When they blew the 300 trumpets, the Lord set every man's sword against his comrade and against all the army. And the army fled. [22]

The characteristics of unity are diametrically opposed to disunity; complete opposites, and certainly much more pleasant! Synonymous with unity are agreement, accord, consensus, peace, harmony, solidarity, unison, assent, unanimity, concord, wholeness and oneness; [23] and unity can be defined as:

- The quality or state of not being multiple: oneness

- A condition of harmony: accord

- Continuity without deviation or change (as in purpose or action)

- The quality or state of being made one: unification

- A totality of related parts: an entity that is a complex or systematic whole [24]

God in His three persons as Father, Son and Holy Spirit is the perfect example of unity:

> God's unity is an incommunicable attribute of the divine essence that refers to the absolute oneness and uniqueness of God (unity of singularity) and to the utter simplicity of his essence (unity of simplicity).
>
> Divine unity is an attribute of God which affirms God's uniqueness and absolute oneness (unity of singularity) as well as the qualitative unity of the divine essence (unity of simplicity). The former implies that there is only one divine being. God is numerically one, not in the sense that he is one among others, but exclusively and solely the one God. All other beings exist from him, through him, and to him. The latter, God's unity of singularity, is the inner unity of God's essence by which all composition is denied. It affirms that in God everything is one; his attributes are identical with his being.[25]

Time and again, Jesus taught of His oneness with Father and Spirit, and their perfect cooperation was displayed after Jesus' baptism:

> *And when Jesus was baptized, immediately he went up from the water, and behold, the heavens were opened to him, and he saw the Spirit of God descending like a dove and coming to rest on him; and behold, a voice from heaven said, "This is my beloved Son, with whom I am well pleased." [26]*

Jesus' prayer for us just before He went to the cross was about being in unity, both with God and with one another:

> *I am praying for them. I am not praying for the world but for those whom you have given me, for they are yours. All mine are yours, and yours are mine, and I am glorified in them. And I am no longer in the world, but they are in the world, and I am coming to you. Holy Father, keep them in your name, which you have given me, that they may be one, even as we are one. [27]*

Back to the concept of good news, our God is good all of the time; furthermore, that never changes and there is nothing in or of Him that can ever be equated as bad:

Give thanks to the LORD, for he is good, for his steadfast love endures forever. Give thanks to the God of gods, for his steadfast love endures forever. Give thanks to the Lord of lords, for his steadfast love endures forever; [28]

Every good gift and every perfect gift is from above, coming down from the Father of lights, with whom there is no variation or shadow due to change. [29]

With both His hope for us and His example in mind, it is helpful to examine the scriptures regarding unity within the body of Christ:

I therefore, a prisoner for the Lord, urge you to walk in a manner worthy of the calling to which you have been called, with all humility and gentleness, with patience, bearing with one another in love, eager to maintain the unity of the Spirit in the bond of peace. There is one body and one Spirit—just as you were called to the one hope that belongs to your call—one Lord, one faith, one baptism, one God and Father of all, who is over all and through all and in all. But grace was given to each one of us according to the measure of Christ's gift. [30]

I appeal to you, brothers, by the name of our Lord Jesus Christ, that all of you agree, and that there be no divisions among you, but that you be united in the same mind and the same judgment [31]

But now that faith has come, we are no longer under a guardian, for in Christ Jesus you are all sons of God, through faith. For as many of you as were baptized into Christ have put on Christ. There is neither Jew nor Greek, there is neither slave nor free, there is no male and female, for you are all one in Christ Jesus. And if you are Christ's, then you are Abraham's offspring, heirs according to promise. [32]

So if there is any encouragement in Christ, any comfort from love, any participation in the Spirit, any affection and sympathy, complete my joy by being of the same mind, having the same love, being in full accord and of one mind. Do nothing from selfish ambition or conceit, but in humility count others more significant than yourselves. Let each of you look not only to his own interests, but also to the interests of others. Have this mind among yourselves, which is yours in Christ Jesus, who, though he was in the form of God, did not count equality with God a thing to be grasped, but emptied himself, by taking the form of a servant, being born in the likeness of men. And being found in human form, he humbled himself by becoming obedient to the point of death, even death on a cross.[33]

A characteristic of every meeting at Aslan's Place is that the attendees have diverse backgrounds; we come from many different denominations, races, cultures and countries; yet we remain in unity. The same phenomenon occurs when many of us gather together independently for Bible studies, prayer groups or just to fellowship with one another. How can this be? It's because we simply follow the lead of the Holy Spirit and work at doing only what we see the Father doing. After all, it worked for Jesus:

So Jesus said to them, "Truly, truly, I say to you, the Son can do nothing of his own accord, but only what he sees the Father doing. For whatever the Father does, that the Son does likewise[34]

Unlike many churches, there is no bickering over doctrine because our standard is strictly the sixty-six books of the Bible. Yes, there is discussion; yes, there are questions; we are very interactive, but there is no disunity. What a blessing!

---

[1] https://www.psychologytoday.com/us/blog/ulterior-motives/201406/why-hearing-good-news-or-bad-news-first-really-matters

[2] Collins Thesaurus of the English Language–Complete and Unabridged 2nd Edition. 2002 © HarperCollins Publishers1995, 2002

[3] Genesis 3:8–13

[4] Psalms 51:9–12

[5] Jeremiah 2:14–17

[6] Proverbs 26:20–21

[7] 1 Corinthians 3:3

[8] Proverbs 6:16–19

[9] Proverbs 16:28–29

---

[10] 1 Timothy 5:13

[11] Proverbs 11:13

[12] John 6:41–42

[13] Romans 1:29–32

[14] Jude 1

[15] Jude 17-19

[16] Genesis 11:1-9

[17] John 11: 47-48, 53

[18] Acts 7:57-58

[19] Acts 18:12-13

[20] Matthew 24

[21] Psalm 68:1-3

[22] Judges 7:9-11a, 13-15, 20-22

[23] Collins Thesaurus of the English Language – Complete and Unabridged 2nd Edition. 2002 © HarperCollins Publishers 1995, 2002

[24] Inc Merriam-Webster, *Merriam-Webster's Collegiate Dictionary*. (Springfield, MA: Merriam-Webster, Inc., 2003)

[25] Gayle Doornbos, "God's Unity," in *Lexham Survey of Theology*, ed. Mark Ward et al. (Bellingham, WA: Lexham Press, 2018).

[26] Matthew 3:16–17

[27] John 17:9–11

[28] Psalms 136:1–3

[29] James 1:17

[30] Ephesians 4:1–7

[31] 1 Corinthians 1:10

[32] Galatians 3:25–29

[33] Philippians 2:1–8

[34] John 5:19

CHAPTER TWO:
UNITY

A good picture of unity is a jigsaw puzzle that has been completed; the chaos that existed when the pieces were dumped out of the box has been resolved, and all of the jumbled parts have come together as a whole to produce a pleasing image. We, both as individual Christians and the Church as a whole, are called to be conformed to the image of Christ Jesus.[1] Apart from Him, our lives are kind of like that unassembled puzzle, a confusion of jumbled parts; but with God, we can become one, individually or corporately, even as God is One.

Paul first discerned unity as a spiritual being August 2018, and he identified two key scriptures. First:

> *And when the priests came out of the Holy Place (for all the priests who were present had consecrated themselves, without regard to their divisions, and all the Levitical singers, Asaph, Heman, and Jeduthun, their sons and kinsmen, arrayed in fine linen, with cymbals, harps, and lyres, stood east of the altar with 120 priests who were trumpeters; and it was the duty of the trumpeters and singers to make themselves heard in unison in praise and thanksgiving to the LORD), and when the song was raised, with trumpets and cymbals and other musical instruments, in praise to the LORD, "For he is good, for his steadfast love endures forever," the house, the house of the LORD, was filled with a cloud, so that the priests could not stand to minister because of the cloud, for the glory of the LORD filled the house of God.[2]*

Notice that the declaration of God's goodness happened in an atmosphere of total unity. The musicians, the priests, and everyone present were in complete agreement; they were of one accord. What truth were they unified around? They were not in agreement about some set of theological or religious tenets; they were unified around one truth, *he is good, for his steadfast love endures forever.* Is this what it means to be unified with all believers, to be of one mind and one spirit? And, is this what it means to be unified within ourselves as individuals? In 2017, the Lord showed us that we must first be in unity within ourselves so that our spirit and soul parts that have been scattered in the length, width, height, depth and in the stars, are returned to us so that we are one in Christ. We cannot personally declare His eternal love when we are not in unity within ourselves, because our wounded parts are in so much pain they are not willing to declare His goodness. The second scripture is:

> *All these with one accord were devoting themselves to prayer, together with the women and Mary the mother of Jesus, and his brothers…When the day of Pentecost arrived, they were all together in one place. And suddenly there came from heaven a sound like a mighty rushing wind, and it filled the entire house where they were sitting. And divided tongues as of fire appeared to them and rested on each one of them. And they were all filled with the Holy Spirit and began to speak in other tongues as the Spirit gave them utterance.* [3]

That first Pentecost marked the public beginning of the early Church with signs and wonders; but notice, it only happened after they gathered together in unity for seven weeks. The word for unity in Hebrew is *echad,* [4] meaning 'one', and it occurs 687 times; in Greek it is *homothumadon,* [5] meaning 'of one accord'. Whether in the Old Testament account of the dedication of the temple, the New Testament account of Pentecost, or in present-day testimonies; whenever unity manifests, the presence of the Holy Spirit in power and glory can be discerned.

Though we've never specifically written chapters about unity, it is a foundational theme in all that we do and flows throughout many articles, books, webinars and generational prayers. Unity is encouraged every time we meet, and it's not unusual when that encouragement is delivered via prophetic words; many more than will fit in this book:

March 2006: A new kind of unity; I am building an army. The first will be last; the last will be first, and not one will be greater than the other.

October 2006: You cannot go back...unity brings a cup of gold and he's going to pour out gold and honey of revelation over us...the angel is pouring gold and honey over us.

February 18, 2008: You are connected by power, power, power...you are to operate in power, godly power...a spirit of unity is here. Practice; learn to operate in unity. There is authority in unity; greater wisdom, greater understanding in you, and you in Me because I have given you a spirit of unity.

August 2008: The network, it is the network; stay close in the network. Unity; trouble is coming against the network and unity is most important...We took a step through the door and do not live by the Greek mindset; it is a new paradigm and new way. We declare that we will walk uprightly before you, united in love in unity.

November 2009: You have made it; the next level of transition is here. It is a position of declaration, a platform of justice. Don't you know you have been positioned for such a time as this? It has been a time of changing hearts and healing souls. There is unity among you, so then you can go; you are under new management.

May 2010, during a time of tremendous trial for Aslan's Place: There's more than meets the eye, there's more than meets the eye; watch your attitude, watch your attitude; pray in unity, pray in unity. Bless your enemies; do not curse them. Be careful of who prays and how they pray. Keep your eyes, your focus, on Me; the I AM, I WAS, and I WILL BE; victory is already yours.

July 2010: For those who call upon my name, I will make a shift. I will make a shift in your families; I will make a shift in your organizations. There will be true connectedness; joined, the way I called you to be joined.

One mind, one heart, one soul; unity of the Spirit, not unity of man.

May 2011: The keys will open evangelistic doors to help people escape the places the enemy has sent them. Unity, unity, unity; unity is the key. This unity is what separates. Authority is in the unity.

September 2015: Unity, unity; it's more than you think. One will put a 1000 to flight. You all are standing on the brink, for the Lord your God will fight for you for you. YWHY, YEHOVAH, ELOHIM fights for you…All are connected by His light; the sound of unity in the Spirit is a good fight. Realms upon realms into the greater heights…For the God of Heaven is with you and near…seek His majesty; seek the King.

February 2016: This is multi-dimensional; get used to it. Unity; unity is in this place; you are connected by life and eternal grace. You've done well up to now, to listen and obey…this is a place of friendship; My friendship, My heart, for I have gathered you here to be in close unity so that when you leave this place you will still be in unity, and you will remember the things I've said here. I will put a deeper understanding within you for you are hungry for Jesus' heart, and I promise that I will fill you up for I love you with a great and mighty love. Ask and you shall receive.

March 2018: A new day, a new beginning; well done, well done. There's a huge celebration. Unity is the key; unity will be the driving force. Without unity it can get derailed. We have to have unity; there's no room for offense or hurt feelings.

October 2018: This is about the perfect bond of unity. Let the peace of Christ rule in your heart, which is complete love and purity. Set your resolve in one body and one mind, and the call to be thankful at all times. Let the word of Christ dwell in you richly with all wisdom, teaching and admonishing with psalms and singing. The power of thankfulness is in your heart; giving thanks to God is where you start.

December 2018: Unity is always in the bond of love. Seek first the kingdom and all else will be done. Forgive those who have been separated as I have forgiven you. Self-forgiveness will make a way to restore and make new. You are changing, so preserve the unity of the spirit in the bond of peace…in truth and love grow up in all aspects of who you are…in the body of Christ being fitted together for the unity of all.

August 2019: You're all together in this plan; unity is at your hand. Submitting one to another will release the decree on earth as it is in heaven for kingdom worth. From the view of limitless provision on how it should be, all has been given to you as you freely receive. Now together you are a well-watered garden producing fruit; heal the man, heal the land for the anointing of truth. I am coming quickly, and that is the perception you should have, changing from old teachings and the paradigms of man. The kingdom is a movement and it never stops. You may know this now but you don't stay here; don't let fear count the cost. Unity is your safety, and wisdom will always be found; the path of righteousness is always peace, so truth will abound.

July 2021:This is a test, so remain in the Lord's rest. The enemy is trying to wear you down but he does not possess resurrection power. The winds of revival are blowing and the enemy is doing everything he can do to stifle the winds. Intercession is key, and maintaining your unity…Fear not; do not be anxious but rest in My provision for the vision.

In August 2009, unity was discussed in a gathering, with several voices chiming in:

You'd be surprised how often it is our perception when we totally misunderstood someone else, so this trying to maintain unity is a tough business. There is a story about the mission of a priest in a South American country who brings the love of Christ to the people. It is paradise, and then the Church comes in, war breaks out, and the whole thing is destroyed. We all get offended so easily. It takes one second, and we get offended because of insecurity and rejection.

That was a major issue in kids' camp. There were numerous incidents with kids fighting in the pool, "I want the raft." The whole week was about practicing unity. We asked them to wear badges of kindness, and the very ones that we were having trouble with were actually hugging each other toward the end.

We all feel unworthy to be able to say something, though it may not be as much of a problem here. A lot of prophetic people have been quiet for so long, and that creates unworthiness. When we hear or discern something, and recognize it is for the Body but hold onto it, we lose the unity that God wants.

Unity is not what we think it is. Just to keep unity, I come into agreement with a lot of crap.

We believe the lie and come into agreement with the lie. Unity is not compliance, and we don't have to enter into agreement with falsehoods.

One thing to keep in mind is that God uses all five of our senses, working together in unity to help us understand what is occurring around us in the physical world; those same senses also operate supernaturally, which is what we call discernment. This ability to tell good from evil and do what the Father is doing is amplified when used in community with others. Each person has unique giftings, and in any given gathering one person may see, another may hear, feel, taste or smell; and each of us knows only in part.

This is why unity is so important in the Church, because when we come together we can test our discernment with one another and our cooperative effort leads to increased understanding. In fact, it is through unity that new revelation is unpacked and understood; it is our journey together that brings enlightenment to the wisdom the Lord is sharing; it is in unity that the mysteries of the Kingdom are revealed. For example, almost every prayer in the Aslan's Place generational prayer manual[6] was developed in unity with one another, sometimes with fifty or more people in agreement. How often do we see that happen? In another instance, the Lord surprised us during a gathering with the initial revelation about the righteous length, which is a place of unity and oneness. How appropriate it seems that new revelation about unity came out of unity!

Have you ever gazed in wonder at an outdoor panorama where diversity comes together in unity? Maybe it was a mountain, a desert, a beach or a forest where different aspects of God's creation came together to paint a beautiful picture of unity? Diverse animals may have scampered about amongst trees, flowers and shrubs of all kinds. It could have been sunny, rainy or snowing, but in unity the display was magnificent. That's what the Church should look like; tall leaders coming together with small warriors, men and women alike dressed in different nationalities and cultures; but all reaching up for the Son, just as a plant reaches for the sun; all growing and serving together in perfect harmony:

> *Behold, how good and pleasant it is when brothers dwell in unity! It is like the precious oil on the head, running down on the beard, on the beard of Aaron, running down on the collar of his robes! It is like the dew of Hermon, which falls on the mountains of Zion! For there the LORD has commanded the blessing, life forevermore.* [7]

---

[1] Romans 8:29, Philippians 3:21

[2] 2 Chronicles 5:11-14

[3] Acts 1:14; 2:1-4

---

[4] James Strong, *Enhanced Strong's Lexicon* (Woodside Bible Fellowship, 1995).

[5] W. E. Vine, Merrill F. Unger, and William White Jr., *Vine's Complete Expository Dictionary of Old and New Testament Words* (Nashville, TN: T. Nelson, 1996), Vol. 2, p. 9.

[6] http://aslansplace.3dcartstores.com/Generational-Prayers--2022-Edition--Paperback_p_615.html

[7] Psalms 133:1–3

CHAPTER THREE:
UNITY ILLUSTRATED

Several years ago during a discussion about unity in a seminar, a man with a degree in mathematics from UC Berkley responded to a comment Paul had made about how one can chase a thousand, and two can put ten thousand to flight.[1] Asked if he could come up with an equation about that, he developed an interactive geometric shape that illustrates on a sliding scale the unity that occurs among 1 one to thirty people.[2]

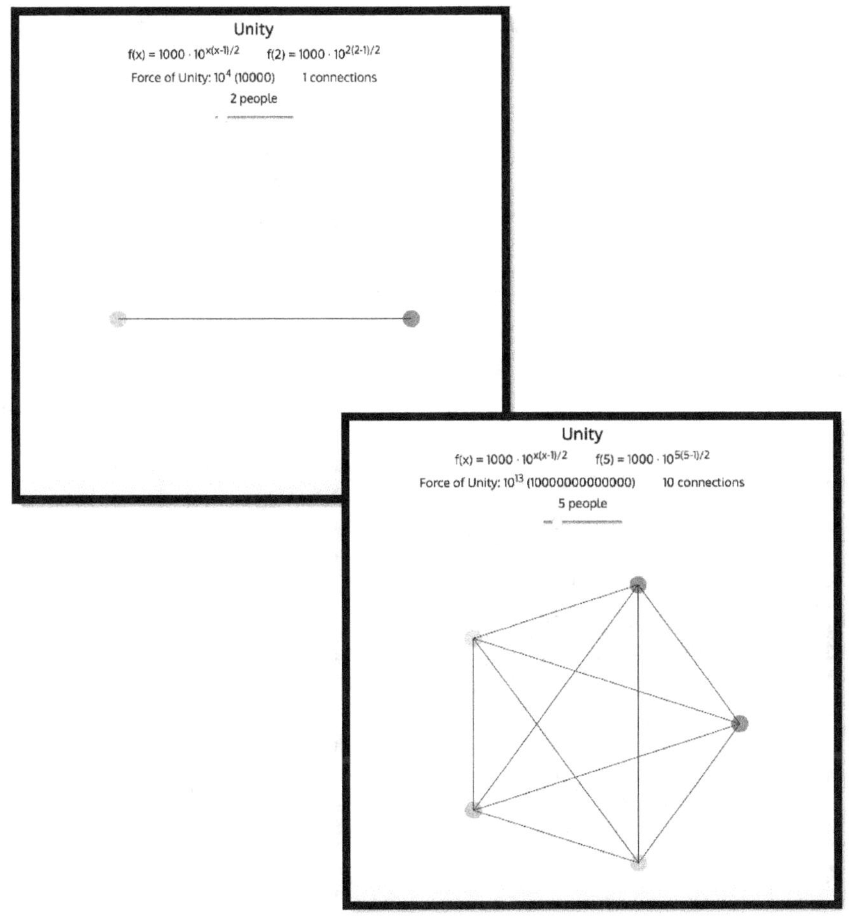

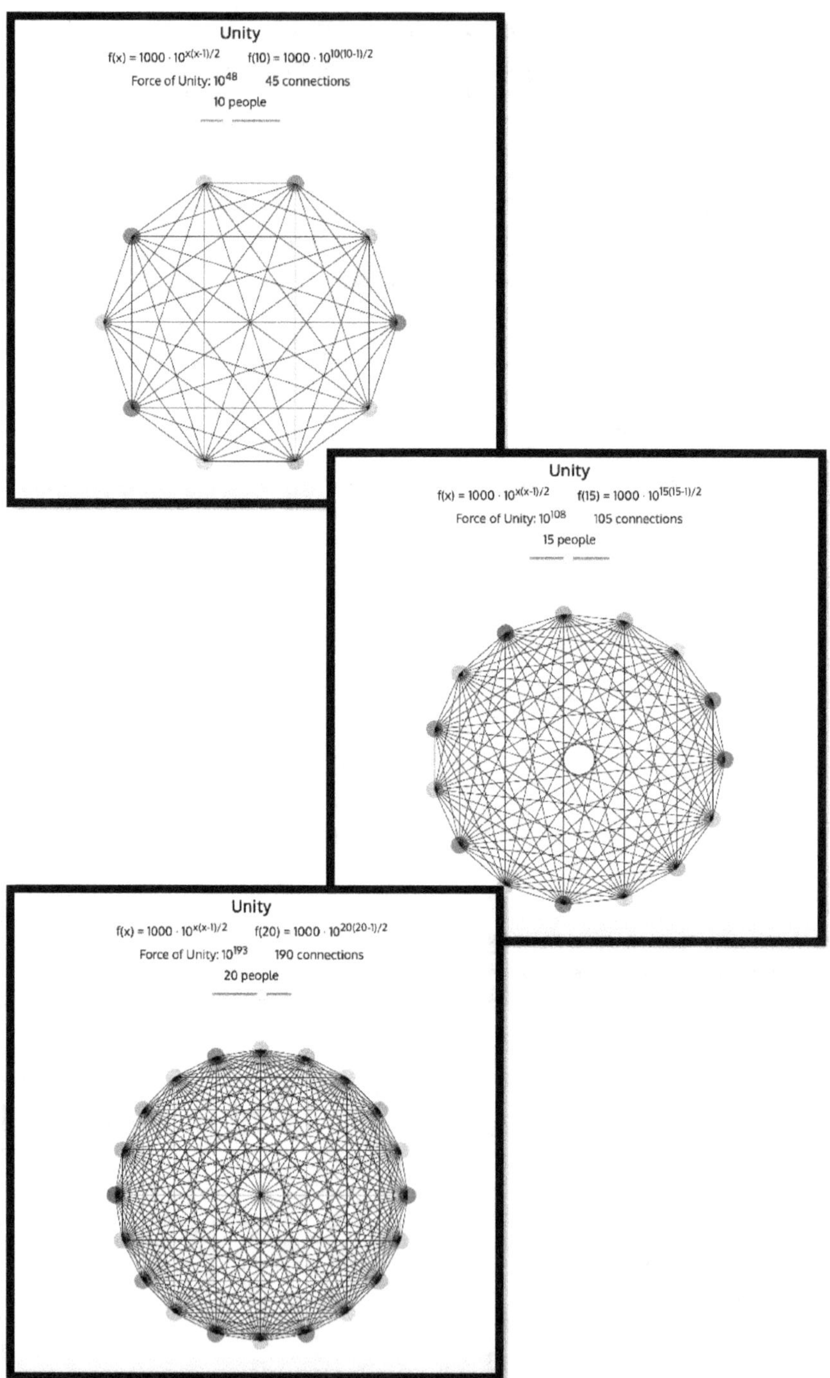
Unity
f(x) = 1000 · 10^x(x-1)/2   f(10) = 1000 · 10^10(10-1)/2
Force of Unity: 10^48   45 connections
10 people
Unity
f(x) = 1000 · 10^x(x-1)/2   f(15) = 1000 · 10^15(15-1)/2
Force of Unity: 10^108   105 connections
15 people
Unity
f(x) = 1000 · 10^x(x-1)/2   f(20) = 1000 · 10^20(20-1)/2
Force of Unity: 10^193   190 connections
20 people

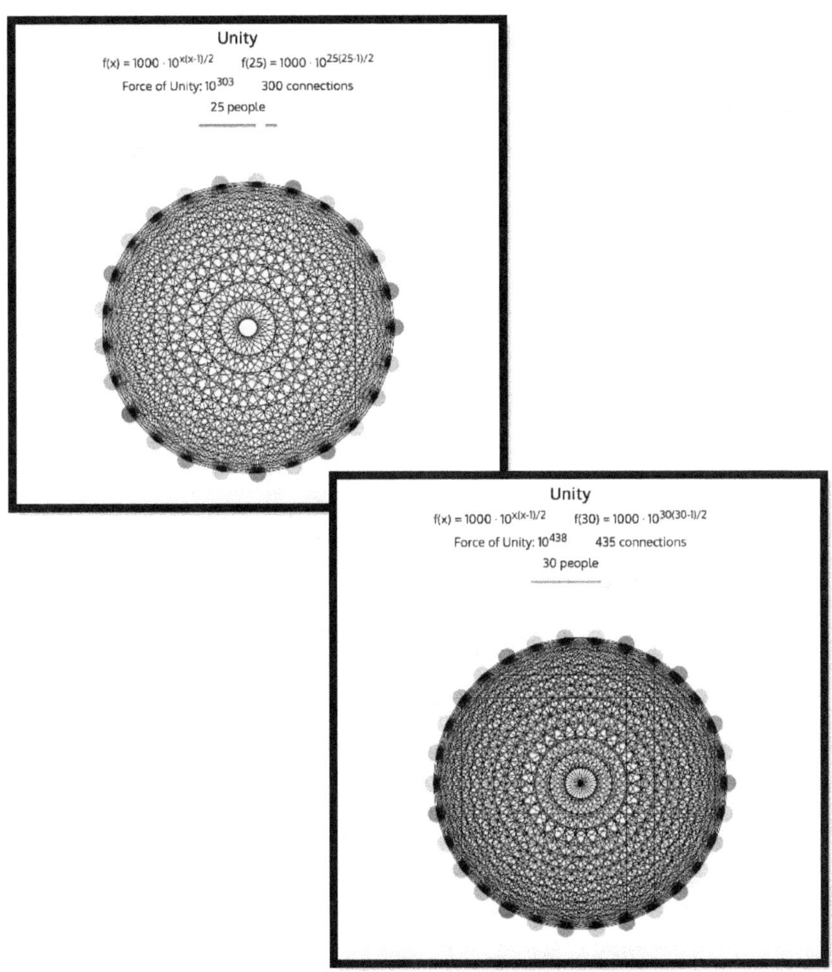

It is often said, "A picture is worth a thousand words." We definitely agree! Clearly, unity among many is a beautiful thing:

Behold, how good and pleasant it is when brothers dwell in unity.[3]

---

[1] Deuteronomy 32:30

[2] Access to the interactive illustration is available at: https://god-equations.herokuapp.com/unity

[3] Psalm 133:1

CHAPTER FOUR:
DEALING WITH OFFENSES WITHIN THE BODY OF CHRIST

Television crime shows have been a popular pastime in my (Brian's) family. Of course, our kids don't watch with us anymore because my wife and I often make snarky comments about the feasibly of the story; and regardless of the story line, we are always looking for justice to be served. We want to see criminals receive the appropriate consequences for their crimes. In other words, we want to see an offender receive justice.

However, this chapter isn't centered around crime; but rather, offense. All too often, when others offend us, we want to see justice served. Perhaps we want to be vindicated and shown to be in the right, or perhaps we want to see the offender receive consequences for their actions. Sometimes the fact that others seem to get away with sinful activities is an offense in itself.

In our struggle for unity in the Body of Christ, offense is a significant adversary. Fortunately, Jesus gives us a wonderful process for fostering unity within the Church, and it is found in Matthew 18:15-17. But, in order to follow this process, we must do so from the right mindset. Let's examine how Jesus illustrates the need for unity throughout the chapter.

Who is the Greatest?
Matthew 18:1 begins with Jesus' disciples asking, "Who is the greatest in the Kingdom of heaven?" In an age where people take pride in their number of social media followers, I suppose it's comforting to see that some things never change. One wonders if, even here in the first century, the disciples were concerned with hierarchy. Or, maybe they were trying to determine who Jesus' favorite was. Another possibility is that the disciples were wondering who would be in charge after Jesus departed.

Regarding the disciple's motivation, Jesus addresses the real issue in Matthew 18:2-5:

> *And calling to him a child, he put him in the midst of them and said, "Truly, I say to you, unless you turn and become like children, you will never enter the kingdom of heaven. Whoever humbles himself like this child is the greatest in the kingdom of heaven.*
>
> *"Whoever receives one such child in my name receives me, but whoever causes one of these little ones who believe in me to sin, it would be better for him to have a great millstone fastened around his neck and to be drowned in the depth of the sea.*

As a child, I remember seeing a painting hanging in a church that depicted Jesus sitting with some children. Actually, the children were more or less on top of Him and they were looking into His eyes. These children didn't seem to care who was greatest; they just wanted to be with Jesus. To me, this painting coveys the point Jesus was making in the passage above. I propose that He was telling His disciples that they were asking the wrong question. They should have been asking themselves, "Am I staying humble and looking to Jesus?"

Safety in Numbers:

As we make our way towards Jesus' process for unity, let's keep in mind that we must stay humble. Focusing on who is right or who is wrong is often a waste of time. Furthermore, there is no need to ponder the concept of rank or hierarchy. After all, we are all equal in Jesus Christ;[1] and by the way, since we are all equal in Christ, there is no reason to go straight to a leader and ask them to fix the behavior of somebody else. We'll discuss this in more detail later in the chapter.

Jesus provided another point for our discussion in Matthew 18:12-14:

> *What do you think? If a man has a hundred sheep, and one of them has gone astray, does he not leave the ninety-nine on the mountains and go in search of the one that went astray? And if he finds it, truly, I say to you, he rejoices over it more than over the ninety-nine*

that never went astray. So it is not the will of my Father who is in heaven that one of these little ones should perish.

Personally I don't relish the idea of being compared to a sheep. Perhaps this metaphor is meant to contribute to our humility. Nonetheless, when I consider that Jesus is the Good Shepherd,[2] I'm content with this analogy.

In the context of this parable, it appears that the concept of one shepherd managing one-hundred sheep is completely reasonable. That's because sheep understand that they are safer when they are together. In other words, their safety increases greatly when they are in unity. Furthermore, there is no indication that the flock tries to block the errant sheep from returning. They instinctively know that welcoming more sheep into the fold increases the flock, and therefore also increases the level of safety.

The problem is, most of us are more like cats than sheep. We each go our own way and then hiss or scratch at each other when gathered together. We need to be more like sheep and welcome others back into the fold. We should never begrudge others when they appear to receive special treatment from our Lord because that special treatment meant they were lost, and the Good Shepherd has gone to find them.

Forgiveness:
Peter's words bring us to another concept regarding unity when he asked:

Lord, how often will my brother sin against me, and I forgive him? As many as seven times?[3]

It's reasonable to think that Peter felt quite generous in suggesting that he forgive seven times. However, Jesus seems to have been nonplussed by Peter's apparent magnanimity and replied with:

I do not say to you seven times, but seventy-seven times[4].

If Jesus made that statement in the twenty-first century, hearing it would lead to a Silicon Valley startup and the development of a smartphone app called 'iForgive'. Then, people everywhere would tally the number of times they forgive, and celebrate when the maximum amount of forgiveness has been reached. However, Jesus was speaking to people who lived in the first century, so we must consider His answer from that point of view. This phrase was considered to be a common saying at that time and meant, 'no limit'.[5] Therefore, those who heard it would have understood that Jesus was giving the directive to continually forgive. Incidentally, this is further enforced by the parable of the unforgiving servant that follows in Matthew 18:23-35.

This brings me back to my opening statement about crime dramas. Often, I find that I'm willing to forgive, but still want to see justice served to my satisfaction; but the reality is that we must also surrender matters of justice over to God. After all, God cannot be unjust, because justice is part of who He is:

> *Righteousness and justice are the foundation of your throne; steadfast love and faithfulness go before you.*[6]

Following His parable of the persistent widow, Jesus made it clear that God brings justice:

> *And will not God give justice to his elect, who cry to him day and night? Will he delay long over them? I tell you, he will give justice to them speedily. Nevertheless, when the Son of Man comes, will he find faith on earth?*[7]

Yes indeed, God gives us justice; but there is no promise that we will be happy with that justice! We must be content in the fact that God measures everything perfectly. In the fight for unity, let us forgive without ceasing, and surrender all matters of justice over to God.

The Right Mindset:
Nestled amongst the passages we just studied is an amazing process from Jesus for dealing with offense. I propose that Matthew 18:15-20 not only lays out a process for dealing with sinners in the body of Christ, but also tells us how to respond when another Christian offends or hurts us. Let's start by looking at the first step:

> *If your brother sins against you, go and tell him his fault, between you and him alone. If he listens to you, you have gained your brother.*[8]

Notice that this verse states we should go directly to the person. We shouldn't discuss what transpired with others, nor should we immediately take the situation to a pastor or group leader. Perhaps you feel either that you need a sanity check or you want to verify your hurt or offended feelings. Well, the first thing you should do is ask God to help you perceive what occurred according to His truth. In fact, it is a great idea to ask God if you should simply let go of the situation. However, if you would like a second opinion, then talk to someone you trust who doesn't know the other person, and don't use names.

If you feel that you need to move forward in this process, then pray and ask God to bless the conversation and go alone to talk to the person. Share what you perceived about the event, keeping in mind this isn't a rebuke. Rather, you are sharing what you perceived. It is important to remain aware that you may have misunderstood what transpired.

If the person listens to you and apologizes or clarifies the event to your satisfaction; then congratulations, you have successfully pursued and maintain unity!

If you aren't able to resolve the situation, then it is time to move on to the next verse:

> *But if he does not listen, take one or two others along with you, that every charge may be established by the evidence of two or three witnesses.*[9]

The idea here is to bring a couple of witnesses with you. These should be people who know both you and the person with whom you have an issue. Even so, they should not be people you've recruited to your side. In other words, the first time the witnesses should hear about the situation is when you are all together.

To give you an example of the conversation, I'll use my name as the subject of the conversation:

> You: "Will you please come with me to talk with Brian?"
>
> Potential witnesses: "What is this about?"
>
> You: "I don't want to give you details until we are together with Brian."

If those you invite press you for details, then they aren't the right people to bring along. Instead, choose two people who understand that you are trying to protect unity.

Once you, the two witnesses, and the person are together, it's time to communicate the situation. One of the benefits of the two witnesses is that they provide an outside perspective on the situation, which means you should be prepared for the others to correct your perspective. If the four of you resolve the issue, then praise God! Unity has been restored.

If the person refuses to resolve the issue, and the two witnesses agree that the issue needs to be resolved, then we move on to the following verse:

> *If he refuses to listen to them, tell it to the church. And if he refuses to listen even to the church, let him be to you as a Gentile and a tax collector.*[10]

Let's begin our discussion here with a review of the word translated as 'church', which in the original Greek is ἐκκλησία, or ekklēsia. This word literally means 'the called', and is used to refer to a church, assembly, congregation. In other words, it is a group that meets together for various political, religious, and civic purposes.[11] That means this process is applicable to any group of believers, not just an institutional church.

To continue with our review, the first time any leaders of the ekklēsia should hear of the situation is when they come together with you, your witnesses, and the subject of the discussion. Even at this stage, be ready for the possibility of personal correction as the leaders prayerfully shed light on the entire series of events. However, if this person is indeed found to be at fault and also refuses to listen to the leaders, then Jesus said the individual should be, "as a Gentile or a tax collector".

This does not mean we should refrain from any contact with this individual. After all, Jesus dined with tax collectors and people whom scripture referred to as sinners[12]. Instead, I propose this means that unless this person repents, they should no longer be permitted to be a participant in regular gatherings with the group.

Why is it so important to put some distance between the group and this person? It is because any person (or group of people) who dishonors the pursuit of godly unity is a threat to the entire body of believers.

Jesus explained the power of godly unity as He continued:

> *Truly, I say to you, whatever you bind on earth shall be bound in heaven, and whatever you loose on earth shall be loosed in heaven. Again I say to you, if two of you agree on earth about anything they ask, it will be done for them by my Father in heaven. For where two or three are gathered in my name, there am I among them.[13]*

When we consider the context, this passage makes it clear that the goal of dealing with sin or offense is not to pursue justice. Instead, it is to keep the fold intact, and to maintain unity in the Body of Christ. Furthermore, there must be agreement to pursue the mind of Christ.

It is only together, as one flock, that we are truly safe; for this is the place in which we enjoy the full protection and intercession of our Good Shepherd, Jesus Christ.

---

[1] Galatians 3:28

[2] John 10:11,14

[3] Matthew 18:21

[4] Matthew 18:22

[5] Owen, J. J. (1864). Commentary on Matthew and Mark (p. 230). Leavitt &

Allen.

[6] Psalm 89:14

[7] Luke 18:7-8

[8] Matthew 18:15

[9] Matthew 18:16

[10] Matthew 18:17

[11] Davis, D. L. (2014). Assembly, Religious. In D. Mangum, D. R. Brown, R. Klippenstein, & R. Hurst (Eds.), Lexham Theological Wordbook. Lexham Press.

[12] Matthew 9:10

[13] Matthew 18:18-20

CHAPTER FIVE:
GRACE: IT'S NOT WHAT I THOUGHT

In 1989, I (Paul) was pastoring a church and had been speaking on spiritual warfare. As a result of that sermon a person came in for prayer, and for the first time demons manifested and we were off and running. For the next two years, if something strange did not happen every week it was a very slow week. In fact, it was usually three or four strange things; and soon pastors, friends, and a therapist began sending us people to pray for. With no real clue about what we were doing, we just did it anyway by faith. Once, a therapist asked me to pray for someone who had Multiple Personality Disorder (now known as Dissociative Identity Disorder); so one Sunday afternoon, five of us gathered together with the client. As we communicated with her, she went to a little girl alter and took on the personality and vocabulary of a three-year-old. Suddenly she said, "Paul, do you want to see her totally healed; I realized the Lord was talking to me and I felt a 'woosh' as well as power on my head. God's power hit the room, and here we were, all these American Baptists who hadn't a clue about any of this stuff! I asked if everybody else felt that and, with eyes as big as saucers, they replied that they did. A bit later as I was getting ready for the evening service, I called my wife, Donna, who was home with sick children, and said, "Something has happened to me and I don't know what it is." Little did I know that was only the beginning!

Something new happened to me recently, which I want to share. My concern in doing so is that often, when you share things that happen spiritually it's like trying to describe the taste of an orange. If I say that an orange tastes like an orange, then I haven't really described how it actually tastes, and even if I say that it's sweet, I haven't done it justice. Sharing this spiritual experience is a bit like that, for while I want others to comprehend the sweetness of the experience it's very difficult to put it into words. Listeners may have a sense of, "Well that's nice for you, but it can't (or doesn't) happen to me;" or perhaps, they either a sense that I am being arrogant or a who-do-you-think-you-are-? attitude. The truth is that I don't know why, but something definitely has happened to me, after which I asked the Lord how this could be applied to everyone else. I don't want things to happen only to me; I want all of us to be able to experience what has happened.

For most of us, our beliefs are based on personal experience, and I am no different. I have preached over 1,500 sermons and, prior to what recently happened, if I were to present a sermon about the power of grace, it would be an intellectual discussion about the Hebrew & Greek meanings of the word 'grace', a look at all the scriptures on grace, along with a discussion of what they mean. It would all be about information; people would take copious notes and, for the most part, go away and forget what had just been learned. Then, sooner or later the notes would be thrown away. But, when you experience something you remember it! As a Baptist pastor, I preached on the gift of healing, but it was all theory; we debated the gift of tongues, but after I started speaking in tongues (much later) I had this startling revelation that everything we truly believe is based on experience. You may say, "I don't believe in tongues" or, "I don't believe in healing"; and when asked why you don't believe, the answer is usually that you have not experienced it. As a left-brain, didactic, expositional preacher, I preached through the books of both the Old and New Testaments; but it was all just doling out information. Then I started having the 'woosh', the first of which was pretty dramatic; and then we had a seminar with Charles Kraft, who came from Fuller Seminary to spend a weekend teaching about spiritual warfare. Our secretary had broken her ankle and the severity of the injury left her with a twisted ankle that had atrophied. The doctor had just told her it was going to have to be amputated, but she came to that seminar anyway. Charles Kraft had brought all these strange people from the Vineyard Church and my son, Brian, suggested that we ask those people to pray for my secretary. I figured it wouldn't hurt anything, so we laid hands on her, and her whole body started shaking; then her ankle transformed right in front of all our eyes, and she was completely healed. All of a sudden, I believed in healing!

I realized that revelation is only information unless it is experienced; then it becomes a reality. As pastors, we give out lots and lots of information, but until the touch of Jesus is experienced, it's just words. You go out witnessing, offering absolutely-true information about Jesus; some people will listen and walk away to forget, much like those intellectual sermons mentioned earlier. Often though, others will make an intellectual decision to accept Jesus, which is a conversion, but when they experience Him all those words suddenly become a reality.

To review, my first 'whoosh' was in 1989. Later, around 1994, a young man came to our gigantic (5 or 6 kids!) youth group, and we were both talking about and experiencing things of the Spirit. The young man just sat there; and told me later that the entire time, he was trying to stop everything that I was doing in the Spirit because he was a fifth-generation Mormon and a practicing Buddhist who often practiced astral projection. He said, "Everything I did would not work against you". After most people had left, we sat down together and I said, "Tell me about Mormonism," even while thinking that this conversation was going nowhere fast. Then I had an idea, and asked if I could try something; he agreed. Though I don't often get a Word of Knowledge, I had a thought and said, "Anger, come forth." As his eyes rolled back in his head and he made a hissing sound, I called him by name and told him to come to the front. "What was that," he asked. I replied, "That's who's controlling you;" to which he responded, "What do I do?" My answer, "You accept Jesus as your personal Savior;" which he did, and I felt the Holy Spirit come into him with a 'woosh', like filing a bag. He went through a knock-down deliverance, with five of us holding him down while he dragged us around the room. But you see, it had just been information until he experienced it.

To share my recent experience is a gigantic leap for me; and if I'd known in advance what would be required to get here I don't think I would have done it. But I am a changed person so, prayerfully, my story may give you hope that something can change in your life.

On May 30, 2020, on Pentecost, we held an illegal meeting in the midst of Covid. The Lord had told us that we were to meet, and I remember sitting in my jacuzzi realizing I could go to jail for having this meeting. It was really a sobering moment as I thought, "I don't think I want to go to jail, but I need to be obedient to the Lord." If you remember Pentecost 2020, all the prophetic words floating around in the Christian prophetic circles indicated that this was to be a gigantic Pentecost; it was expected to be like the first Pentecost, complete with signs and wonders. A dozen or so people came, some from very far away, and all were ready for the light show to begin; but nothing happened, at least not for them. But a very prophetic friend was there, and she came over and said, "Is it okay if I stand in front of you?" I replied that it sounded all right to me; and then she said, "The Lord is going to do a deliverance on your DNA. The power of God hit me so hard that I was thrown back in my seat, unable to move. Some people left very angry, accusing me of not doing what the Lord wanted, because there was supposed to be power there. I said, "Well, I felt it! I'm stuck in the back of my chair and I can feel a deliverance coming off of me."

Again, this is like trying to describe what an orange tastes like! When I first started doing deliverance, I felt, saw and heard nothing; I would sit down and people would manifest. That was my great gift! We'd have people all around the clients, and they would get words of knowledge, and they began feeling things on their body. But nothing would happen to me at all, until a couple years later in 1991, when the church invited me to leave after a wonderful series of 3 meetings. You see, Baptists love meetings; they love conflict and debate; they love a good fight, so bring it on! More people attended those business meetings than came to church regularly. In the end, I resigned from the church, after which I started feeling something on my head. From then on, I'd be driving along or just going about my business, and it would feel as if things were clapping on my head. The best description is that it was like a moving headache all the time; I knew it was evil, so I'd tell it to get off. Then, as I prayed for people the headache would return, and I understood that I was feeling the evil coming off of them.

Sometime around 1996, a friend called from Alaska and said, "Paul,

I have this verse for you that says that with one word Jesus cast them out. Do you know what that means?" I was afraid I did, so I started saying the word and would lock into people in such a way that I could feel deliverance coming off of them; and sometimes it would go on for seventy-two hours—three days!—and it was 24/7. After a while, that changed and I would feel the deliverance only until I went to bed that night, which was still very difficult. Sometimes it was so dreadful that no one in the house could sleep because deliverance was ongoing; it was just terrible, and there were times that I'd literally be on the floor in pain. This is not a complaint; I'm just trying to set up what happened to me on that Pentecost evening, when my friend stood in front of me and said that the Lord was going to clean out my DNA. The next day I woke up and could feel a violent, moving headache coming off of me, realizing that I had been doing this for thirty years. Now, it continued for three, four, five and then six days; so when a friend who is an internationally known prophet called, I said, "This is not stopping." He replied that it was going to continue for fifty-four days. I disagreed, "Oh no, it's not; I can tell you it's not going to go on that long." My thinking was that Daniel fasted for twenty-one days, so maybe three weeks would do it; but nope, twenty-one days passed. Surely then, it would not go past forty days; but forty days became fifty-four days, and Isaiah 54 became relevant.

The deliverance stopped for a few days as the Lord gave us new revelation; but then it started up again, and went on and on and on, for weeks and weeks and weeks. During that time, Donna and I had two previously scheduled week-long vacations; and I thought, "Lord this is not fair; I'm on vacation but I wake up every morning feeling all this stuff coming off my head." As my friend had initially prophesied, I could feel the Lord removing evil off my DNA and RNA; I could also feel ungodly thrones being removed, and the windows of the heavens being realigned. It was constant, and was wearing me out every day. Still doing ministry, the deliverance I felt was not the client's but my own. I was trying to live a normal life with my wife, doing the everyday stuff we have to do; but it was very, very exhausting.

Meanwhile, the Lord gave us revelation about the mighty ones, the deep darkness, the kings, and the firmament; but every time there was more revelation, there was also more deliverance. I really thought, "I cannot live like this anymore; will this ever end?" If this was how my life was now going to be, how could I even function?

July 1st arrived, and I'd had a prophetic word that something was going to happen then. Suddenly, my deliverance stopped, but as I was driving around I could now feel deliverance coming off the land. I thought, "Here we go again; it's not coming off me anymore, but it's coming off the land." Another friend had given me a word earlier, saying that there was something important about July 4th being more than just the nation's Independence Day. She was right, for on July 4th there was a gigantic shift, and I felt a new sensation on the back of my head; it was grace; I was in both the Realm of the Firmament and the Realm of Grace. After that, when I prayed for people and someone else on the prayer team would complain about how bad it was, I'd be thinking, "It's not that bad." I'd finish the prayer session and immediately find myself back in the Realm of Grace.

Then I had the idea to determine how many days there were from May 30, 2020/Pentecost, to July 4, 2021/Independence Day, and discovered that it was four-hundred days. How significant, because 400 is a number that often signifies captivity; it is the number of years that Israel spent in Egypt. In comparison, praise God that my experience only lasted 400 days!

Later in July 2021, as Donna and I flew to Hawaii I discerned that we were in the Realm of Grace. Then, as this message was preached there at Mountain View Community church in Kaneohe,[1] we were still in the Realm of Grace. You see, it is all about the power of grace; for grace is not only God's riches at Christ's expense, which is wonderful information; but grace is also a place of power, a place of supernatural power in fact.

A night or two after my initial encounter in the Realm of Grace, I was lying in bed pondering grace and I was reminded of two verses:

For by grace you have been saved through faith. And this is not your own doing; it is the gift of God, not a result of works, so that no one may boast.[2]

This mystery is that the Gentiles are fellow heirs, members of the same body, and partakers of the promise in Christ Jesus through the gospel. Of this gospel I was made a minister according to the gift of God's grace, which was given me by the working of his power.[3]

I realized that grace is a power word, and I had to get up, turn on the light and get a Bible so I could look at 2 Corinthians 12:9-10, which is where Paul quoted Jesus' words, *My grace is sufficient for you, for my power is made perfect in weakness.* As a Baptist, we'd talk about how that's such a nice thought; and it is true, but you see it's not to be only about information because it is the experience of a place where we can live in His grace. What kind of power is this? It's an amazing power; it's the power that enables me to not feel deliverance all the time; it's God's strength made perfect in our weakness enabling our testimony to be like Paul the Apostle's as his testimony continued:

"Therefore I will boast all the more gladly of my weaknesses, so that the power of Christ may rest upon me. For the sake of Christ, then, I am content with weaknesses, insults, hardships, persecutions, and calamities. For when I am weak, then I am strong."

When I am weak, I am strong because of the place of grace, the heavenly Realm of Grace. So I began studying some of the words, focusing first on the concept of grace being 'sufficient' or *arkeo*, which is a philosophical Greek word meaning contentment, a state of happiness and satisfaction; not information but experience. Aristotle believed that happiness involves a cognizant component of information, a philosophy that the Church seems to have adopted since it expertly doles out an abundance of information. Later philosophers emphasized disciplines of living that are supposed to enable us to dispel the things that bring unease to our lives. What a bunch of gobbledy-goop! Information alone will never produce relief, and while I do love discussing what the Word of God means, we need an experience in which one understands who one is, and recognizes and excels in respect to rightly ordering oneself. It's time to experience the power of God!

I have developed a virtual friendship with a philosopher who taught that subject at a Catholic university. He's done some prayer sessions with me, and I have also done some discernment coaching with him. During the last session, he was experiencing power surges as we talked. As I was exploring this topic of grace and sufficiency, I called him and asked about the bottom-line purpose of philosophy. He quickly responded that it is to gain knowledge, so I asked what the emotional purpose of philosophy is. He became really quiet, and then said it's contentment. You see, contentment is a state of rest and peace; it's a place where I have no more need because His grace is sufficient so that I am content despite the cares of the world.

I went through years and years of high anxiety before into entering into the place of God's Rest; and now, entering into this Realm of Grace, I find that it is sufficient, just as Jesus promised. If anyone is experiencing high levels of stress, anxiety or discontentment, be encouraged that there is a place of sweet abode near to the heart of God; it's an experience that you can enjoy.

During my 400 days of deliverance, I could discern the windows of the heavens, as mentioned in Malachi 3:10. The New King James Version says that the Lord will open the windows of heaven and pour out such blessings that there will not be room enough to receive it. The English Standard Version says, *until there is no more need."* I realized at the end of the day on July 4th that the windows were all now aligned.

I remember my first prophetic dream that Donna was in, sometime around 1990; she was a patient at the Montclair hospital, where she gave birth to a deformed child. A nurses' cart was there, and I saw what looked like double mirrors with fractal images. (If you've ever seen a room with two mirrors, such as a bedroom, or barber/beauty shop, the mirror reflected in front of you appears to become smaller and smaller. In the Spirit, I'd always thought they were spiritual mirrors, but I realize now that they are windows. In my dream, all of the windows were totally aligned, which is what I feel now, so that there is no more need. Also in the dream, something happened and the deformed baby was instantly healed and I heard, "All the babies are healed; it's sufficient and there is no more need; strength to the 7th power," which is God's *dunamis*.[4]

We've had a lot of amazing experiences in Hawaii, not the least of which occurred in 2014. On a Tuesday, as I was praying for a person who had come for ministry, I felt something very strongly and said, "I don't know what this is, and I don't think I am supposed to do anything right now." The client then started vibrating under the power of God, and many wonderful things happened. Meanwhile, Hurricane Anna was approaching and we were getting ready for the storm. It was supposed to hit on the west side of the islands, zeroing in at Waikiki; just imagine the storm surge that was expected to affect all of the hotels and devastate the beach. By Saturday night, water was everywhere, but all of a sudden the storm started averting 120 miles off of Oahu. By Sunday morning, we were sitting in church with a wonderful light rain falling. The amazing thing is that Anna means grace, and it was clear that the Lord's grace fell on us.

I called a Jana Green and said, "Something has happened to me." She replied, "I see golden pipes on the back of your head." So, look at Zachariah 4, which I have taught about for a long time; but there is a center section that we had only talked about, but never experienced.

> *And the angel who talked with me came again and woke me, like a man who is awakened out of his sleep. And he said to me, "What do you see?" I said, "I see, and behold, a lampstand all of gold, with a bowl on the top of it, and seven lamps on it, with seven lips on each of the lamps that are on the top of it. And there are two olive trees by it, one on the right of the bowl and the other on its left." And I said to the angel who talked with me, "What are these, my lord?" Then the angel who talked with me answered and said to me, "Do you not know what these are? I said, "No, my lord." Then he said to me, "This is the word of the LORD to Zerubbabel: Not by might, nor by power, but by my Spirit, says the LORD of hosts.*

> *Who are you, O great mountain? Before Zerubbabel you shall become a plain. And he shall bring forward the top stone amid shouts of 'Grace, grace to it!'"*[5]

I love that Jeremiah didn't have a clue what that was; he sounds a lot like us! But moving down toward the end of the chapter:

> *Then I said to him, "What are these two olive trees on the right and the left of the lampstand?" And a second time I answered and said to him, "What are these two branches of the olive trees, which are beside the two golden pipes from which the golden oil is poured out?" He said to me, "Do you not know what these are?" I said, "No, my lord." Then he said, "These are the two anointed ones who stand by the Lord of the whole earth."* [6]

This is exactly what I was feeling on the back of my head—two golden pipes that would boil with the oil, because the oil is the anointing of the Lord. This is, *Not by might, nor by power, but by my Spirit, says the* LORD *of hosts…amid shouts of 'Grace, grace to it!* Grace, which means 'favor' is right there; it is about the power, not the information.

---

[1] Sermon Link: https://soundcloud.com/user-923681474/august-01-2021?utm_source=www.mvcchawaii.org&utm_campaign=wtshare&utm_medium=widget&utm_content=https%253A%252F%252Fsoundcloud.com%252Fuser-923681474%252Faugust-01-2021

[2] Ephesians 2:8–10

[3] Ephesians 3:6–7

[4] See Strong, J. (1995). *Enhanced Strong's Lexicon.* Woodside Bible Fellowship.

[5] Zechariah 4:1–7

[6] Zechariah 4:11–14

CHAPTER SIX:
EVIDENCE OF THE POWER OF GRACE

For our fortieth anniversary, Donna and I went on a cruise in the Mediterranean Sea. I should have asked the Lord first though, because I had to fast for three of the ten days on the ship. Having to fast on a cruise should not be permitted or allowed! When we arrived at the port of Rome, we joined a bus tour that stopped at the cathedral of St Paul, the one stop of the day. Clearly, it was a very important stop as we all made a bee line to the bathrooms; and I was very annoyed because I had been fighting against evil the entire time since docking at the port, continually trying to cast it off. It was dreadful! But about halfway to the bathrooms, I hit a wall of power, and 'woosh', everything was gone. I was wondering, "What is this, at a Roman Catholic church no less?" I told Donna to check it out, asking, "What is this? What is all this power doing here?" Then I went into the cathedral and ran into the power again, still wondering what in the world was happening. Then I noticed a sign right there in front of me, "The burial place of the Apostle Paul," and I thought, "He is really buried here and the anointing remains! Instantly, I understood something that Paul wrote:

> *And I, when I came to you, brothers, did not come proclaiming to you the testimony of God with lofty speech or wisdom. For I decided to know nothing among you except Jesus Christ and him crucified. And I was with you in weakness and in fear and much trembling, and my speech and my message were not in plausible words of wisdom, but in demonstration of the Spirit and of power, so that your faith might not rest in the wisdom of men but in the power of God.* [1]

I get worked up about this, because we've made the Church all about talking, while refusing to engage in the power.

After resigning from the church, I began having many experiences with the power, though it was still quite a mystery to me. I'd become the interim pastor of a church around October 1991, and soon I found myself thrown to the ground under the power. I had no frame of reference for this! The power experiences in Toronto had not happened yet, and wouldn't until 1994. I didn't know anything about being slain in the Spirit; after all, I was an American Baptist for goodness sakes! When the power hit me, I was thrown to the floor while waves, and waves, and waves of power flowed over me for over an hour. It was like one of those rides in an amusement park where they spin you around and you're forced back against the wall, unable to move. Visiting with a friend of mine, he walked into the power and we both hit the floor, blasted under the power of God. I said, "I don't know what this is, but I like it." Finally, I managed to get up and get in the car to go back to the place I was staying; I had a Vineyard tape playing, and I started worshipping when, 'woosh'; and I thought, "Lord I have to drive here." This has happened many times since those early days, so often that it doesn't matter anymore as I've routinely flopped about on the floor under the power of God with many friends.

After we moved to the high desert, more adventures began. We were visiting a church where our friends led the worship. We didn't know the pastor, and just went to watch. I sat down in the second row, and all of a sudden was plastered against the seat, thinking, "I don't know what I am doing here." I managed to go somewhere—I don't know where!—for the entire service, and when it was over and I knew that I was supposed to pray for the pastor. I did know the associate pastor, so he went and found the pastor, who came over and I asked if I could pray for him. He agreed, so I laid hands on him, and he shot off like a rocket, right into a stroller. Everyone in the church was panicking, but he came for dinner the next night, bringing his wife and children, and we had a wonderful time. However, he never talked to or looked at me again.

Then I was invited to speak at another church that we were attending, and I started 'cooking' in the Spirit during that afternoon. I called the pastor and said, "Donna and I have to talk to you because I just want to warn you something might happen tonight." He responded that he'd seen just about everything, so we went to the church. They were singing a worship song with the lyrics, "Lord, do with me whatever You want to do." I thought, "Oh, don't sing that; please do not sing that song." The pastor then told me to just give my sermon and then he'd dismiss anyone who wanted to go, after which I could "do my thing." We did that, and by the time it was over, his eyes were expressing without words, "I've never seen that before!" He never made eye contact again, so we left that church.

I spoke to another church in the area, and there was so much power that I was literally hanging onto the pulpit, but nothing happened afterwards. It seems that the Lord was ready to release His power in the high desert, but the churches weren't willing to receive it.

My friend, Rich Marshall, has a television show *God At Work* on God TV, and I was in Florida where we were taping two shows for his program. While there, I met the pastor of a four-thousand-member church in a large city. He asked me to pray for him, and as I did we both ended up doing a little spin about ten times, and he went down on the ground. He then said, "I'm going to invite you to come to my church." I thought, "That's not going to happen," but he did invite both Rich and I to come, and I was to speak on Saturday to the business leaders in the church. Sixty to seventy people attended and we had a wonderful time. On Sunday morning Rich was speaking in two services. The worship was so amazing that Donna and wanted to go back to the second service and experience it again. As we sat in the front row. I was just sitting there minding my own business when I discerned the arrival of the angel of the city. Angels are messengers and this one was no exception, so while I'd met the pastor and am a friend of Rich, I had no assigned part in this service; so I went over and told Rich, "The angel of the city is here and has a tongue and a message." He answered, "What are you going to do about that?" I reply, "I'm not going to do anything, because this is not my church nor my responsibility today. I'm just coming to let you know so you can decide if you want to do something about it." I sat down, trying to behave myself, and the pastor introduced Rich, who went up front and stopped to talk with the pastor. I had this fear inside of me that they were talking about the angel, and then the pastor said, "Paul, would you like to tell the people what is happening right now?" Now, the sanctuary was packed with 1,500-1,700 people and I was thinking, "No, I do not want to say anything." But, I went up onto the platform and said, "I believe the angel of your city is here and there is a tongue and a message." The pastor did the unthinkable and said, "Let's get the message." Sitting down, I was thinking, "Oh no, please." As one lady got up and began speaking, I said to Donna, "Nope, that's not the message," so when the lady finally finished we were happy about that. Another lady stood and went off into a tongue, followed by the interpretation; and as power of God fell on that room, Rich, the pastor, and I were rolling around on the floor, and I zoned out. All around I heard screaming, and people were falling out into the isles. Pretty soon, the worship team got up and began singing and I heard the pastor say, "Paul, why don't you come back," so I dragged myself back to the seat and from there laid my hands on people. Bam! They'd go down, people were still screaming, and deliverance was taking place. Then the pastor said, "Everyone that wants to be saved come forward." Remember, there's been no sermon and no discussion, but over twelve people responded to receive the Lord. Church was now over and he dismissed everybody. They politely escorted Donna while I was dragged into another room, and we have not heard from them since. Given our history, is it any wonder that I wasn't enthused about the angel with the message?

It also happened in a church in Hawaii. I was to speak one night, and there were about 300 people present. I remember standing at the door thinking, "I don't know what I'm going to do." You generally have the just-in-case talk ready, but my goal is to always simply follow the lead of the Spirit to do what the Father is doing. After the service began and someone from the front row said, "I see a golden lavar," I realized the Tabernacle was there. I hadn't taught about that for years, but here we were having a Bible study on the Tabernacle. Then I had the thought that we were to walk through the Tabernacle and discern the various furnishings, though we'd never done that before. I stationed the pastor's wife at the Holy of Holies, and people walked through. There were power surges and people were falling everywhere. I watched, thinking that this was amazing. The next day, I found out that four young single men had come to service that night and had walked through the Tabernacle. One of them said, "I don't know what happened in there but demons left me." The next day, all four became Christians and then were baptized. The following Sunday, several leaders left the church, along with many of the members. You see, many do not want God coming to church; He just messes up the program and shakes people up.

In January 2021, my son, Brian, and I were invited to the San Francisco Bay area by my first intern at Aslan's Place, who is a school principal. We were to pray for, teach, and train a group of home-schooled elementary students. I was concerned because I had been discerning the Father's power for two days, so I called my friend before we went and said, "I want to warn you; something may happen, and if you don't want us to come we won't, because I am done with churches where people don't want the power. Don't blame me later if you still want us there." He replied that he did want us, so we got ready to leave, and on the morning we were to drive to Northern CA, I could still feel the Father's power. I called my friend again and said, "I got these words, 'Get ready, get ready, get ready. Do you still want me to come? Because if you don't, I'm fine." He reaffirmed we should come so off we went, eventually arriving at the old elementary school that they rent, which is straight out of the 50's. The plan was that we would meet first with the board and a couple of teachers, and later that Thursday evening with the parents and some of the kids; then, on Friday we'd be with the kids all day. As we sat there on Thursday, I got the phrase and asked the question, "Are you ready to become the landing strip for the power of God? Because if you do not want this, I don't care; I have nothing to prove here, and this is not my school." We continued and everyone was talking when Brian said, "You have not answered my dad's question." It became very quiet as they soberly considered, and then they all said yes. I said, "Do not blame me for what might happen because I don't know what is going to happen. I'm not in charge here." I proceeded to give a short talk to about fifty adults and kids, and then said, "I believe there is a gate of power here because I feel the Father's power, and I believe that something is going to happen tonight; but if you as teachers and parents are not going to steward the power with these kids, then we will not continue because it would be a big mistake." I was very serious, but they agreed to proceed.

I felt a gate and a 10-year-old boy got up; I asked if he could feel the gate. He touched the gate and, bam, he was down on the floor in an open vision. I thought, "This might work!" We finally got him up and he walked through the gate, all-the-while screaming and carrying on under the power of God. Everyone else started walking through as well, and they were also screaming and carrying on. Eventually, I turned to my son and said, "I think this is getting out of control. What are we going to do here? They are all going off the rail—parents, teachers and kids." I finally got everyone up and holding hands, and said, "We are going to need to learn to walk in the power." The next day, we did some teachings on discernment from 9AM to noon; and by the time the clock got to 12, the kids (who ranged from kindergarten to 6th grade) were getting really squirrely, so along with a few adolescents and adults it was clearly time to break for lunch. But first they asked, "When are we going to walk thru the portal?" I hadn't said anything about a portal! When we came back, I felt the Holy Spirit as Wisdom and I realized that there was a gate of Wisdom. First, we talked about the Holy Spirit and about Wisdom; then the first kid walked through and hit the ground again. Everyone walked through the gate and suddenly all these squirrelly kids are lying on the floor and all we heard for the next 30 minutes was, "Aaahhh, aaahhh." I realized that I had never seen such supernatural power in my life. Imagine, a group of elementary school children; you haven't even touched them, yet they are quietly resting under the power of God in His presence, and experiencing open visions. Since then, their principal has been stewarding their gifts and the kids are growing in the Spirit. Watching in amazement as those kids laid there on the floor under God's power for over a half hour, I thought, "Isn't it ironic that all this happened in the San Francisco area?"

Years earlier in the early 2000s, I had been in Zurich, Switzerland where we had a conference. The Pastor came up to me and said,

"Paul, there's talk in the town, and they do not want you here." A sense of holy indignation rose up in me, and I became so angry in the Lord that I wrote a Declaration: [2]

> I do not come to you with excellency of speech or with man's wisdom to declare to you the testimony of God. For I'm determined not to know anything among you but Jesus Christ and Him crucified. I come in weakness and fear, and in much trembling. My speech and my preaching are not with persuasive words, but in demonstration of the Spirit and power so that your faith will not be in the wisdom of men, but in the power of God.

> I am determined to know Jesus Christ and the power of His resurrection, and the fellowship of sharing in His sufferings, becoming like Him in His death.

> I declare that the Kingdom of God is not a matter of talk, but of power.

> I declare that we have this treasure of power in jars of clay to show this all-surpassing power is from God, and not from us.

> I declare my goal is that the God of our Lord Jesus Christ, the Father Glory, may give to you the spirit of wisdom and the revelation of the knowledge of Him, and that the eyes of your understanding may be enlightened that you may know what is the hope of His calling, what are the riches of the glory of His inheritance in the saints, and what is the exceeding greatness of His power to us who believe, according to the working of His mighty power, which He worked in Christ when He raised Him from the dead and seated Him at His right hand in the heavenly places.

> According to the Word of God, I stand against all who have a form of godliness but deny its power.

> I stand in the name of the Lord Jesus against every and all

religious spirits that seek to confuse, disrupt or misinterpret what I say.

I declare that only the Lord God can create spiritual gifts. The enemy can only distort, twist, and pervert what God has already created.

I declare that it is time for the Church to take back all spiritual gifts stolen by the enemy, and allow the Holy Spirit to use them for the sake of the advancement of the Kingdom of God.

I declare that everything I do during our time together is in submission to the Lord Jesus Christ and the leadership of this conference (or church), and that I do everything in the name of the Lord Jesus Christ whose blood was shed on the cross for us, and who rose from the dead and is seated at the right hand of the Father.

I declare that His is the kingdom, and the power, and the glory forever. Amen

Flying from CA to Hawaii, I heard the words, "This is a revolution." But, what is a revolution? It's a revolt against the status quo, which is something that many of us agree is necessary. So then, what do we do and where do we start? The Lord showed me it's time to start a revolution, and gave me eight statements defining it as:

1. A revolt against complacency in the Church; in order to establish radical obedience to the Lord

2. A revolt against the Church's order of service; in order to establish Holy Spirit directed worship

3. A revolt against doing what I want to do; and believing what I want to believe, in order to establish true submission to the commands of our God, as presented in the Word of God, the Bible

4. A revolt against fear and anxiety; in order to establish a declaration that I will remain on the Ancient Path, which is unwavering acknowledgment that I will trust in the Lord

5. A revolt against wavering opinions that lead to an unstable life; in order to establish a stable mind, which is always at rest

6. A revolt against constantly ignoring what the Lord wants to do; in order to establish a lifestyle that sees and hears what the Lord is doing, and is always ready to do what He wants to do

7. A revolt against a cultural belief that I have the right to get anything I want, need or expect; in order to exchange it for the biblical truth that I'm to deny myself, and to take up the cross and follow Him

8. A revolt against the belief that God has no power; in order to fully embrace in power of God to bring dynamic and dramatic change to us personally, to our marriages and families, to our cities, states and countries, and to our world

It is time for a power revolution; time to say to God, "We will no longer reject Your power in this place, in this city, in this state, in this country, in this world," and then you don't reject the power. We must agree that He is God, He can and will do what He wants to do, and He will have His way in His Church. Our part is to listen to Him, and we may go weeks and never see His power, but we will always be in obedience to what He is doing. We will always stop what we are doing to do what He is doing; that's what it means to have discernment.

Someone said to me that my gift is really generational prayer, and I got really angry about that and replied, "That is not true! My gift is discernment, and the purpose of discernment is to know what the Father is doing." So, our purpose is to be doing what the Father is doing no matter what we think about it; caring only what He thinks, while caring not at all what anyone else thinks. It is important that the leadership within any group of believers be in agreement that He has the right to do whatever He wants, no matter what it looks like, because when there is unity in the Spirit amazing things can happen. It really is time for something to happen so that lives are changed, people are saved and discipled so they can become all they were created to be. It's time for each one to fulfill their purpose in Heaven and on the earth.

I was in Kingwood, Texas when the Lord gave me this phrase, "For the King and His Kingdom." What do I live for? I live for the King and His Kingdom; everything I do is for the King and His Kingdom. It's not my life anymore; I no longer belong to myself, and it's not about me, what I want to do, or where I want to go; it is about the King and His Kingdom. That's what it is all about, Realms of Grace, Peace and Rest, He is the One doing what He wants through us. It's all about His power, the power for which they eventually crucified Jesus; but shortly before that happened He was at Gethsemane and a cohort of 600-800 soldiers came to arrest him. They asked, "Are you Jesus?" He answered, "I am," and they all fell to the ground.[3] That's power! It's not a matter of talk or of perceived earthly authority; rather, it's all about the power of God .

> *For I am not ashamed of the gospel, for it is the power of God for salvation to everyone who believes, to the Jew first and also to the Greek.*[4]

---

[1] 1 Corinthians 2:1–5

[2] Biblical references: 1 Corinthians 2:1-5, Philippians 3:10, 1 Corinthians 4:20, 2 Corinthians 4:7, 2 Timothy 3:5

[3] John 18:6

[4] *The Holy Bible: English Standard Version.* (2016). (Romans 1:16). Wheaton, IL: Crossway Bibles.

Chapter Seven:
The Sound of the Lord

Preface:
This chapter is taken from a sermon that Paul Cox preached at Rob Gross's church in Kanehoe, Hawaii on August 8, 2021. Since then, God has continued to direct them to develop the Kingdom Institute, which now offers college-level courses both at Aslan's Place in CA, and Mountain View Community Church in Hawaii.

Message:
Our son, Brian, and I have been working together for some time; I submit to him and he submits to me. Brian interprets what I'm saying; I travel to wherever I go in the heavens; and as confused people sit scratching their heads, he brings my message back down to earth so they can understand. He also is gifted at putting the things I discern into a biblical context and will often say both in private and public meetings, "Dad, I don't know about that; let's talk about it." We've learned to work together in unity and it's a great joy. Such mutual submission is biblical, within both our families as well as in the Body of Christ.[1]

With that in mind, it now seems apparent that Rob and I need to model something for you, because church meetings must no longer be just about the person in the front, but about all of us together in unity. In this case, it's about Robert and I working together in unity, so he has the right to interrupt with his own comments or a suggestion that I clarify something. I might also respond to Rob, "We'll get to that pretty soon," and he will undoubtedly just smile and yield the floor back to me.

This part of my talk is very hard on my wife, Donna, because for her to re-visit the past is like experiencing PTSD from our many years of very traumatic experiences. It was very difficult when the first church we pastored rejected the power of God and invited us to leave. We went to a second church, which rejected His holiness; oh, they wanted to experience His power, but they didn't want to live in a holy and righteous set-apart-from-the-world manner. The Lord dealt with that, and it was not pretty; in fact, when I finally resigned after a series of terrible meetings, the Lord told me I was not to argue with them but to simply take a stand. Tragically, three weeks after our resignation, the church, which had over $300,000 in the bank, closed. Clearly, the Lord judged the church and it was found wanting. It was quite terrifying to watch! Next, we moved to the high desert and things deteriorated rapidly.

After more years in ministry, we finally arrived at a point of total discouragement; life seemed hopeless, and things only became progressively worse. I remember the day that Donna dropped me off when I had to go back to work, teaching as a substitute teacher (previously, I had taught eighth grade in a public school for three years). I was terrified to do this even though, ironically, I made a remarkable $75 a day, which was amazing at that time.

One day, Donna and I were sitting on the bed and I asked, "Shall we just stop? Shall I find a permanent job?" Then I got the phrase, "We do not know if we're wrong if we stop;" so with that high-level motivation, we kept on going. There were times when I considered erasing everything off my computer, thinking that the material would never be needed again. But the Lord was relentless as He kept downloading more revelation, more revelation, and even more revelation.

Then a friend told me, "The Lord says that you can go across this bridge or you can jump." It was a no-brainier and I said, "I'll jump." I'm always willing to jump, but I did have a serious conversation with the Lord, "Ok I'm willing to do all this crazy stuff and learn all these crazy things; they are all biblical, but where's the beef?" I used to ask, "Where's the beef?" all the time, meaning I'd do what He was asking but I was looking for results. I didn't want to be involved in a bunch of esoteric, mumbo-jumbo New Age stuff that doesn't help anybody, thank you! Then, one time I was somewhere on the East Coast and a lady came to me and said, "I have a word for you; the Lord said, 'I'm going to show you the beef.'" I laughed out loud because I had never told anyone about that before.

As we went along, the Lord would give us little indicators to pay attention to something new. A clear example was when we were with a friend who had been suffering with Crohn's disease for a long time, and we'd prayed everything we knew how to pray for his healing. He had been on the Toronto Airport Church worship team and had all the high-power healing people praying, but he was not getting healed. It was at the point that he could hardly eat anything and life had become very, very difficult. We were in a meeting north of Toronto when the power of God fell on the room; we were all rolling around on the floor as I reached over to my friend's stomach and said, "Lord, close these doors." Immediately he was healed, and I was thinking, "We might be onto something here." This led to great insights from the Lord, which led to the subsequent revelation of the doors, gates, grid and the dimensions. What's interesting though, is that I would teach this and people would go off and see wonderful results, but I didn't personally see anything more because it seems the Lord is always pushing me forward; push, push, push, push, push! At Aslan's Place, we used to do School 1 and School 2, as well as an internship program, but everything quickly turned into exploration. Soon, School 1 was anything but elementary, and School 2 was very advanced. We finally stopped doing any meetings for a while because no matter what I did the Lord was always pushing us higher and higher. Just imagine poor Donna having to live with me, because as He pushes me into more revelation it is often accompanied by some very strange physical manifestations of discernment. He downloads more and more, and I say, "Ok, Ok, Ok," meanwhile writing everything down. At this point that I've collected thousands of pages of revelation.

We are now on the verge of something new that I'm going to share; I have not yet seen the evidence, but there are all kinds of indicators that we are onto something big. The early church experienced signs, wonders and miracles, right? We've been looking for that, and even seem to be on the cusp of them being poured out. I've had this idea; I think the early church could be compared the feast of First Fruits, and we are finally coming into the harvest with what's happening today. It's as if the Lord is saying, "Okay, I did this in the early Church so you can see what can be done, but now I'm going to show you why it's being done. I'm going to show you how everything works so that you no longer have gunshot prayers where you try to cover everything at once. Instead you can come in with a rifle prayer that hits the bullseye on the target and nail the booger. There will be no contest, because the enemy knows you have clearly identified what the problem is." This is where we're going.

It's like a water distiller we have at home because I'm a tea connoisseur, and like distilled water with my tea because of the pure tea taste. Every day our distiller produces gallons of distilled water, and I'm like that distiller right now. I've had all this information pouring into me; and just this week I've had people calling, emailing, and texting more and more revelation. I couldn't believe that it's all about what we're going to do tonight. I try to distill this all down so that it first makes sense to me and then to you, and we're going to get into some very, very complex stuff. It's the most amazing revelation I've ever received and I like it a lot; but I once again want to say to the Lord with great reverence, "Lord, we'd like to see the beef, because we want to see people healed."

After my recent message on grace,[2] Rob found relevant scriptures that shocked me because it became clear that grace is the key to understanding the power of God:

> *And with great power the apostles were giving their testimony to the resurrection of the Lord Jesus, and great grace was upon them all.[3]*

> *And Stephen, full of grace and power, was doing great wonders and signs among the people.[4]*

> *But the unbelieving Jews stirred up the Gentiles and poisoned their minds against the brothers. So they remained for a long time, speaking boldly for the Lord, who bore witness to the word of his grace, granting signs and wonders to be done by their hands.[5]*

Isn't this astonishing? The context of grace is healing, signs and wonders; and we are discerning that we're now in the Realm of

Grace.

As I started distilling all of this, some of us were at the very-anointed California Pizza Kitchen after church when one person told me that I have a key for one of the men. Immediately, I realized it was tied to vibrations, and later spent a full day going through hundreds of pages of notes about vibrations, distilling much-longer words down to illustrate how vibration, or sound, is a key.

In 2015, I was on a call with a friend who is a composer and a musician in the London Theater when he realized that he had been taken into the righteous deep and felt healing. A gate was discerned, and he felt a vibration and heard a sound; a key was received, and when the gate was opened the vibration stopped. The key was called Grace! Six years passed before I had the revelation about grace on July 4th 2021; the key was grace, and I discovered other words over the years that finally led to the current understanding:

> December 2018: A reformulation of the vibration is the healing for regeneration. All sound is aligned to the great I AM. I am removing the dissonant, for the renown of the Kingdom which is at hand. Great and awesome is this place where glory was organized with power to give faith and grace; and this is a place where you agree with the re-creation of how it was meant to be.

I'm sure you've heard that the definition of insanity is doing the same thing over and over again, while expecting a different result. That is exactly what we've been doing in the Church, repeating the same thing over and over again. We are continually seeking the Lord to discover the key to understanding why we are not getting any better, yet we haven't accepted that all of the spiritual gifts are present and active within the Body of Christ.

> June 2012: There is a seat, there is a sound, a vibration to change and shift mindsets and thought. Come out of the contaminated religiosity that is the mixture of man. There is a sound, a vibration, to bring you into you; the

frequency of Heaven to replace the domains of darkness. We welcome the harp of David, profound deep secrets and mysteries; rhythms of His grace, of His face; authority, the sound of authority; the Spirit of Might wedding with authority.

September 2011: From my heartland to your heartland; catch a wave, catch a wave, catch a wave, catch a wave; a new vibration for the next generation. Receive the grace from the king's face for a new race.

Many of us have had wave dreams, but is this a play on words? It's not only a wave, but also a vibration wave. What grace! Isn't this astonishing?

Beginning in 2005, a friend from Canada had a word three different times regarding Hawaii. She said, "There is a key, there is a key, there is a key in Hawaii in a pawn shop. Redeem it." A pawn shop is a place of redemption, and we actually went to a pawn shop to try and find the key; but the poor guy was so scared because he thought we were the cops.

Let's recall what our composer friend said in 2015, "The key is grace," ten years after the lady kept telling us to, "Find the key, find the key!" Within the same word from 2005, the woman also said to look for berries where there are no berries. I thought, "What are you talking about?" But that part of her word also now makes sense. We moved into our house in 2011; then in 2012, my brother, who is a professional landscaper, offered to landscape our backyard and wanted to put in a vineyard. We bought bare-root vines, and one day I was looking out from where I was seated and noticed there were berries growing on the bare roots, which had not even been planted yet. I talked to a lady with a degree in vineyard management and she said, "That is absolutely impossible," and the next day the berries were gone. As the berries-where-there-are-no-berries word had come to pass., so had the word about finding the key. As the years passed, more relevant words continued to arrive:

August 4, 2007, in Hawaii: There is a key to unlocking the

mysteries of the Kingdom. One spirit, one body, one flesh; Father, Son, Holy Spirit.

March 20, 2009: Crack the DNA code; crack it, crack it. I'm giving you a key to crack the code. Numbers, vibrations, colors and frequencies are all parts of the code that was written. The enemy knew what he lost so he defiled the sound, vibrations, light and frequencies. It is a symphony of defilement.

May 17, 2009: I synchronize you into My time, colors, spectrum, vibrations, rhythms, sounds. You will beat with My beat, march, dance, harmony. Waves and waves are coming; it is His voice, His sound, His vibrations. The seven-fold spirit is in the light; there is a color in each of the spirits; together it is white light. There are healing properties in the light and the colors. Feel healing; the key to healing is in the light and in the colors, which are all connected to vibrations.

September 27, 2014: Does not Wisdom hold a key, a sound to reveal the One who sees?

What in the world does this all mean? Through the gift of discernment, I have a physical reaction to spiritual things, and I can discern on an individual that:

- There is a musical chord made up of three notes tied to everything

- Each chord is made up of three spiritual beings called stars

- The last note seems to be dissonant (reference the above word from December 2018), and we know that one-third of the stars fell

- The chord is in a sphere, which seems to be a spiritual being called a power

- There are two spheres, one male and one female

- These two spheres seem to be connected to the spiritual constellation, Pleiades (Amos 5:8, Job 9:9, 38:31)

Keep in mind that we have the physical stars in our three dimensions, but we also live in the heavenly places, so there are multitudes of other dimensions. In those dimensions are spiritual things going on that mirror what's happening in our physical world. We grew up praying The Lord's Prayer, "Thy Kingdom come, thy will be done on earth as it's in Heaven," but in the original language it actually refers to 'our Father who is in the heavens'; everything we know/experience on the earth is mirrored in the heavenly dimensions.

Look at some spiritual context for the stars:

- Isaiah 14:13 teaches us that Satan tried to ascend above the stars; so we know that stars are high-level spiritual beings

- Revelation 12:7-11 says not that one-third of the angels fell, but one-third of the stars fell

- In Revelation 9:1, it is a star being that gives John a key to the bottomless pit, not an angel, which is part of the reason why we confuse the two; the original Hebrew and Greek are different for both spiritual beings, as is indicated in many different scriptures in the Bible

- Judges 5:20 says the stars went to war at the gates of Israel against the Canaanite kings

In *The Passion Translation*, Psalms 19:1 declares:

> *God's splendor is a tale that is told, written in the stars. Space itself speaks his story through the marvels of the heavens. His truth is on tour in the starry vault of the sky, showing his skill in creation's craftsmanship.*

Space itself speaks—that's sound—His story every day in the heavens, which is plural. Incidentally, throughout the Old Testament, everywhere the word 'heaven' appears it is always plural in the original language, no matter what the translators may say. *His truth is on tour in the starry vault of the sky showing his skill and creation's craftsmanship.* Verses 2-4a continue:

> *Each day gushes out its message to the next, night by night whispering its knowledge to all—without a sound, without a word, without a voice being heard, yet all the world can hear its echo. Everywhere its message goes out.*

Whispering without a voice being heard! That's sound; that's the stars singing, and His sound is all around us all of the time.

In 2nd Chronicles 11:11-14, we read about the dedication of the temple by Solomon, and are told that all the musicians (120 of them) came together with all the singers as one, making one sound. What happened when the sound came? The glory of God filled the temple; it was the sound of unity for they were all in one accord.

In Daniel we have further insights into sound:

> *"I saw in the visions of my head as I lay in bed, and behold, a watcher, a holy one, came down from heaven…The sentence is by the decree of the watchers, the decision by the word of the holy ones, to the end that the living may know that the Most High rules the kingdom of men and gives it to whom he will and sets over it the lowliest of men."*[6]

> *Then I heard a holy one speaking; and another holy one said to that <u>certain</u> one who was speaking.*[7]

That word, 'certain' in Hebrew is *palmoni,* and *palmoni* is a holy one, or a watcher. Some time ago, the Lord told us that the holy ones are the judicial branch of the divine government, and as it is in the physical realm, the other two branches are executive and judicial. We believe that the watchers are the police force of the judicial branch; here on earth we might call them marshals, such as are present when one goes to court. As in the physical, it seems true that the holy ones/marshals of the heavenlies are involved in making declarations and carrying out the court's orders. Long before we realized this function, the Lord had revealed the *palmoni* to us and showed us that they vibrate 444 Hertz, which is the key of A above middle C. Actually, 440 is what every orchestra in the world is tuned to, so there's the concept of sound again.

Recently while discerning the holy ones, it felt like they were delivering thousands upon thousands upon thousands of declarations instantly, like speed-of-light fast, and they were righting a multitude of wrongs because we were confessing, repenting and pleading the blood of Jesus Christ. Note that Revelation 12:11 says that they overcame by the blood of the Lamb and by the word of their testimony. 'Word' in that verse means to give testimony in a court of law about what has happened to you, your family, people you know, and even people you do not know; this is all legal, and is taking place among the holy ones. I don't know if all the holy ones vibrate (I've never thought about that before), but I do know that *palmoni* does vibrate.

I came across this amazing prophetic word:

> The Godly watchers (holy ones) are for you; they stand guard for you, they protect you. But what can they do for you? When you think judgmentally you let out a vibration, a sound, a color; and every cell of your body releases negative vibrations and colors.

New Age people understand this, but they try to adjust everything manually because they are not going to the right source for help. They don't understand creation law, so instead of going to the Creator who can easily adjusted them spiritually (the first step being salvation), they seek help from evil sources. The word continues:

> The sound is warped; take seriously the Word of God. It's your thoughts, your heart, what is in your heart; it's your heart's effects on other people. You're in line with other people whether you believe it or not; and you have power, you have power, which is the power of your thoughts.

We are talking about the truth of the Bible that as a man thinks in his heart, so is he;[8] so not only do our words carry power, but so do our thoughts.

I had a dream many years ago that I could not figure out. I was up against the wall and the Lord was speaking to me. I could not see Him but could hear him say, "Your blood pressure is 197." I replied, "But I'm not under pressure." He said, "It is about your thinking." Once awake and wondering what He meant by that, the thought came that it was about Job 19:7, where Job complained that if he cried out concerning wrong, he was not heard and there was no justice. But that's not true, whether we're talking about Job's thinking or our own. In the same way, we also experience the effects of negative words because by speaking them we are releasing negative vibrations, which produce dissonance in our bodies. This is part of what is true, though not the only thing going on because there are also generational issues to deal with, and it all gets very, very complicated. But then I recalled the scripture:

> *The law of the LORD is perfect, reviving the soul; the testimony of the LORD is sure, making wise the simple; the precepts of the LORD are right, rejoicing the heart; the commandment of the LORD is pure, enlightening the eyes; the fear of the LORD is clean, enduring forever; the rules of the LORD are true, and righteous altogether.* [9]

God's Word is perfect in every way; it leads us to into His truth and His ways, changing the simple into the wise. God's laws always lead us to into truth, causing changes in our thinking, and my dream was about the fact that I needed to adjust my thinking.

Other prophetic words had come through the years regarding frequencies and vibrations; words that we definitely did not understand when they were first received:

August 2006: Paul, get ready. There is a key coming; it is a bigger key; there is going to be a bigger key to tear down bigger systems. There are watchers, vibrations that are steadily increasing; apostles of discernment, bells, sounds, whistles; many keys to many hearts.

October 17, 2009, before the discernment revelation of the stars: See my stars that I have created; hear their voice, hear their sound; they radiate My light, they vibrate with Me. It is one note, one chord, one vibration; one note, they sing together one note; it is the sound of my creation; they sing in unity, they sing in harmony. This is what I have called you to do, and I have given you the keys to healing.

May 2012: You have been waylaid in the past by the enemy, who has deception as a scheme. It is designed to wear down the saints by familiar sound, which is where the ungodly watchers have the key that has kept the saints in a cycle of defeat.

June 2012: The watchers are aligned with authority that goes in and out. Color isn't empty where frequencies go in and out; vibration is what it's all about. Many frequencies make up a color; they go in and out; the color is tied to the frequencies to know who you are; it is the divine plan. As a man thinks by desire within, how he perceives positions him. The greater authority is within. Learn more from the assertive one, Palmoni, for the frequencies of Heaven are the frequencies of the Son.

2012: There's a new breed of healer rising up with sharpened discernment of a key. Discern to execute the generational healing, mentally and physically. There will be a new vibration to bring into the mind of Downs Syndrome, Multiple Sclerosis, Fibromyalgia; the brain waves will come into a new alignment of healing and wholeness. There's a wave coming; there's a wave of healers rising up.

Friends, do you know what the issue is? It is that we are demeaning one another; we are not in unity; we complain, we gripe, we carry on; and all the while that we are speaking dissonance, the enemy is running with it. The enemy claims to have legal right to come against you because of what we're doing, what we're saying and what we're thinking. We do not have the unity that we should have.

When we were at Downey First Baptist Church, I would sing in the choir in the tenor section. I did not say I sang well, but I did sing in the choir. We practiced a piece of music that has become my favorite worship song; *Hallelujah* from the Mount of Olives by Beethoven.[10] Over the years, I've loved playing it often, to the point that I've actually wondered if it was a compulsion or some kind of disorder. Then a few months ago I had the thought that this is probably what Beethoven's body, soul, and spirit was singing to the Lord, and he simply wrote down his personal symphony to God. Possibly, he will continue singing it throughout eternity. This is my opinion: I believe that each of us is also a symphony to the praise of His glory. Isn't that an exciting thought?

When I discern the stars while praying for people, the Lord is gracious to re-tune the dissonate note so there is harmony. We believe this sound holds a key for healing, and *The Prayer to Release the Joyful Sound* is available in Appendix One as well as on our website[11] to help others do the same thing. Another helpful action is to pray Psalm 29 as a declaration:

> *Ascribe to the LORD, O heavenly beings, ascribe to the LORD glory and strength.*
>
> *Ascribe to the LORD the glory due his name; worship the LORD in the splendor of holiness.*
>
> *The voice of the LORD is over the waters; the God of glory thunders, the LORD, over many waters.*
>
> *The voice of the LORD is powerful; the voice of the LORD is full of majesty.*
>
> *The voice of the LORD breaks the cedars; the LORD breaks the cedars of Lebanon.*
>
> *He makes Lebanon to skip like a calf, and Sirion like a young wild ox.*
>
> *The voice of the LORD flashes forth flames of fire.*

The voice of the LORD shakes the wilderness; the LORD shakes the wilderness of Kadesh.

The voice of the LORD makes the deer give birth and strips the forests bare, and in his temple all cry, "Glory!"

The LORD sits enthroned over the flood; the LORD sits enthroned as king forever.

May the LORD give strength to his people!

May the LORD bless his people with peace![12]

Postscript:

During an academy at Aslan's Place in January 2022, Paul taught about the Sound of the Lord. Several musicians sang the note they were hearing, and the power of God was tangible in the room.

The last prophetic word Jana Green sent to Paul was two months before, on November 23, 2021, and it pretty much summarizes the impact of the Sound of the Lord:

> Paul, this is probably what you already know, but I feel it's important for you and Rob to be prepared and informed.
>
> Listen for the shifting; can you hear it? It is here. The sound of healing and recovery is breaking frequencies that hold systems in place. It's turning back consequences that time has made. Important point: there's an intermediate connection that will change direction like a river in flow; an opening for more, the apostolic will restore.
>
> The nations are shaking and you will see rulers fall. The systems of the kings are being unraveled, but the thrones have power that is still involved.
>
> It is what is familiar that men keep. They earned and traded its misrepresentation of what truth should seek.

What happens in the high desert will also connect to Hawaii, don't be frightened; the changes for this are the birthing of the recovery design.

This is the true justice system coming in place. To judge for justice; this is an apostolic mandate. I AM rising up the bride like a redeemed remnant, to possess and recover the divine intention. This is like Ezekiel, who took a lock of hair; put it in the fold of the garment; the remnant shift is here! Many are called in this river to be the true judges of recovery. Apostolic river will bring about unity.

You are this one, make no mistake; your relational network will make a greater way.

Hawaii is set for change. It will be radical. Be patient, it's on its way!!!

---

[1] Ephesians 5:21

[2] Transcript available at https://aslansplace.com/language/en/encountering-grace/

[3] Acts 4:33.

[4] Acts 6:8.

[5] Acts 14:2–3.

[6] Daniel 4:13,17

[7] Daniel 8:13.

[8] Proverbs 23:7

[9] Psalm 19:7–9.

[10] https://www.youtube.com/watch?v=5ZKWcn7bqsQ

[11] https://aslansplace.com/language/en/joyful-sound/

[12] Psalm 29:1–11.

CHAPTER EIGHT:
THIS PRESENT BATTLE

Preface:

This chapter is taken from a sermon that Paul Cox preached at Rob Gross's church in Kanehoe, Hawaii on February 13, 2022.

Message:

Many decades ago, when I was a young man I would often go into my father's library. My dad was a cook in the Marine Core who loved the Bible; he would also collect books and I would read them. One of those books was *Gleamings in Joshua,* by Arthur W. Pink. If my memory serves me correctly, I was going on a backpacking trip and took the book with me. Reading it, I was stunned, and became enthralled with the book of Joshua; it's still my favorite book of the Bible. It's an amazing account of type and antitype.[1] Joshua, as the type, is an Old Testament prophetic indication of Jesus; the antitype would be Jesus himself in the New Testament. In the OT Hebrew, Joshua translates as Joshua, but in NT Greek, it means Jesus. The Book of Joshua is about entering into the land by means of crossing over the Jordan River; and 'Jordan' means to spread judgment, so you pass through judgment but it doesn't touch you as you enter into the Promised Land.

The difficulty is that we Christians, especially in the evangelical world, believe that we enter the Promised Land, set up camp, and then just study the Word while we await the second coming of Jesus. That is not the message from the book of Joshua; rather, it is a call to battle. Recently, I heard the Lord say, "You are to speak to the troops, because this is a call to battle." Keep in mind, I would not vote for this if I could vote! None of us want to go into battle, but as Christians we have two options; we are either the victims, or we are the warriors. Sadly, most Christians seem to want to be the victims. My son had a deliverance session with a lady who had cancer and she actually said, "It is God's will that I have cancer." She absolutely refused to battle for healing, because she believed everything was God-ordained so she was supposed to just live it out. Too many Christians believe that this is the way life is; we just have to suffer through it, and life stinks. But that is not what God has called us to; He has called us to battle.

I was so impacted by *Gleamings in Joshua* that my first sermon was on the first chapter of Joshua. I had become a member of the First Baptist Church in Downey, California in 1966, which was the beginning of the Jesus Movement, though I didn't know that until many years later. When I attended there the first time, I was stunned; I had never heard preaching, a choir, an organ and a pianist like that, and I was intrigued by the church. Already trained to be a schoolteacher, I started teaching eighth-grade history, English, and reading in a public school in 1967. I remember sitting in the balcony of the 2,000-member church and thinking I heard, "You're going to preach from that pulpit." I was so astonished by the power of the preaching of our pastor, Harold Adams, that to have such a thought was absolutely ludicrous. But sure enough, the day came when I delivered that first sermon to 500 people.

At the time, I was the director of the Junior High Department, which grew to about a hundred. Later, I became the director of the children and College Department, with about 60 leaders under me; we had a gym, and were very busy. In the College Department, my first lessons were also from Joshua. Next, I became pastor at the First Baptist church in Buhl, Idaho; and the Book of Joshua became my first sermon series. The pattern continued, first as the pastor at Bethany Baptist Church in Montclair, California, and later at Bethel Christian Fellowship in Chino, California. Once we moved to the High Desert, my first sermon series was again from the book of Joshua. Now, here we are at Mountain View Community Church in Hawaii, and a call to battle from Joshua is very fitting.

When Joshua was told by the Lord to first take Jericho and then the land, I don't think he had a full understanding of the cosmic battle he was engaging in, even though he already knew that there were giants in the land. Friends, this is not just a Bible story; there is actually skeletal evidence of giants throughout the world, ranging anywhere from eight to thirty-five feet tall. This is not theory; this is not made-up stories in the Bible; this is true, verified, scientific fact. Think about this: there were probably close to a million men (maybe as many as three million people in total), moving across the Jordan River and getting ready to go into battle against Jericho, which means 'City of the Moon God'. Incidentally, Allah is most likely the moon god. This many people headed into battle must have been a terrifying thing! I have never been in the military, even at the height of the Vietnam War. Subsequently though, I've read books about it and have had terror come upon me as I thought, "I came so close to going into that battle."

Battle, as we've seen it portrayed in movies, is not all fun and games. Even so, when war breaks out young men are normally very excited. They may think that they are going off to save the day, and coming back as heroes; but then the reality and the terror set in.

My son and I were watching *Saving Private Ryan,* and about halfway through the movie I left the living room because the horror and terrible nature of battle was so excruciating that I couldn't watch it visually. Battle is terrifying! I mentioned that Joshua did not have a full understanding of the Battle of Jericho because he was in a physical battle, which in retrospect seemed very easy, didn't it? But the victory occurred because the Lord is the One who fought for Joshua, and He remains the One who battles for us. Jericho was defeated by a bunch of guys marching around for seven days and blowing trumpets only because it was God taking down an evil people.

I was wondering what Eisenhower said to the troops on D-day (the same year I was born). This is called 'The Order of the Day'. Can you visualize the warriors getting ready to land at Normandy in France, knowing that many of them would die? Imagine the terror of that. This is what Eisenhower said to them:

> Soldiers, Sailors, and Airmen of the Allied Expeditionary Force!

You are about to embark upon the Great Crusade, toward which we have striven these many months. The eyes of the world are upon you. The hope and prayers of liberty-loving people everywhere march with you. In company with our brave Allies and brothers-in-arms on other Fronts, you will bring about the destruction of the German war machine, the elimination of Nazi tyranny over the oppressed peoples of Europe, and security for ourselves in a free world.

Your task will not be an easy one. Your enemy is will trained, well equipped and battle-hardened. He will fight savagely.

But this is the year 1944! Much has happened since the Nazi triumphs of 1940-41. The United Nations have inflicted upon the Germans great defeats, in open battle, man-to-man. Our air offensive has seriously reduced their strength in the air and their capacity to wage war on the ground. Our Home Fronts have given us an overwhelming superiority in weapons and munitions of war, and placed at our disposal great reserves of trained fighting men. The tide has turned! The free men of the world are marching together to Victory!

I have full confidence in your courage, devotion to duty and skill in battle. We will accept nothing less than full Victory!

Good luck! And let us beseech the blessing of Almighty God upon this great and noble undertaking.

I believe we have now crossed over, and we are in the land. At our Aslan's Place academy on Friday, January 28, 2022, a prophetic word was delivered that we are both Joshua and Joshua's army. When I arrived here, an intercessor for Aslan's Place said, "Jericho is about to fall." I say now that we will accept nothing less, Lord, than full victory against the evil cosmic enemies.

So, we are going into battle, but against what? What is it for which we are fighting? Something true about a battle is that when you're a warrior in a conflict, nothing else matters; it's because you are now under the authority of the Commander in Chief, and you will do what exactly he says. When I go into battle, my focus must be on the fight itself, as well as on offering support to those who accompany me. I cannot act against or undermine them, because it could cost me my life. The troops are not the problem; it's the people who complain and gossip in the background. In any battle, the army must have a leader, a general. When the Lord (the Commander in Chief) was initially speaking to Joshua about Jericho, He dealt first with His general, who then instructed his officers. On my birthday, I received a card with both a prophetic word and the verse with which the Lord encouraged Joshua:

> *Have I not commanded you? Be strong and courageous. Do not be frightened, and do not be dismayed, for the LORD your God is with you wherever you go.* [2]

Often, those of us who are leaders did not sign up for this; we were assigned. I've asked my friends, "Who signed up for this?" If I knew what I was going to have to go through, I would not have done it so I am no hero; but I have my assignment and you have yours.

Look at God's instruction to Joshua regarding the nature of the battle:

> *Moses my servant is dead. Now therefore arise, go over this Jordan, you and all this people, into the land that I am giving to them, to the people of Israel. Every place that the sole of your foot will tread upon I have given to you, just as I promised to Moses.* [3]

With that in mind, what is the nature of our battle? First, we are to take back the physical land. Notice that the Lord used the word, 'foot'; so there's a possibility that Joshua lost a foot in battle at some point, and only had one. The land they were to take back was the promised land. Fast forward to today. Have you heard the lies in the media about Israel taking the land from the Palestinians? Not true! While God loves the Palestinians, the land belongs to Him. It is believed that the Garden of Eden was in Jerusalem, and if you trace the order of Melchizedek, which can be done through the Dead Sea Scrolls, it goes from Adam in what would later become the city of Jerusalem, to King David in a direct line. The land has always belonged to the Lord, and we needn't be shy about that. It's as simple as this, many people don't want the Lord to have His land and we are in a battle to take back the land, which causes conflict.

A friend I often work with says, "This is all about the land"; and God wants the land of Hawaii back. Look at His continued instruction to Joshua:

> *Only be strong and very courageous, being careful to do according to all the law that Moses my servant commanded you. Do not turn from it to the right hand or to the left, that you may have good success wherever you go. This Book of the Law shall not depart from your mouth, but you shall meditate on it day and night, so that you may be careful to do according to all that is written in it. For then you will make your way prosperous, and then you will have good success.*[4]

I think Joshua must have been terrified. We must also know the Word and live by it, and this applies to all of us. Next, Joshua commanded his officers:

> *"Pass through the midst of the camp and command the people, 'Prepare your provisions, for within three days you are to pass over this Jordan to go in to take possession of the land that the LORD your God is giving you to possess.' "*[5]

Note that he mentioned the tribes. We understand that Mountain View Community Church is a tribe, and it takes many tribes to possess the land. As Rob and I lead the Kingdom Institute, we are training the tribes. There's nothing wrong with being a tribe, a family, and we must know that victory is the only option. Joshua continued:

> *"Remember the word that Moses the servant of the LORD commanded you, saying, 'The LORD your God is providing you a place of rest and will give you this land.' Your wives, your little ones, and your livestock shall remain in the land that Moses gave you beyond the Jordan, but all the men of valor among you shall pass over armed before your brothers and shall help them, until the LORD gives rest to your brothers as he has to you, and they also take possession of the land that the LORD your God is giving them. Then you shall return to the land of your possession and shall possess it, the land that Moses the servant of the LORD gave you beyond the Jordan toward the sunrise."* [6]

Victory is the only option, and at the end of it is rest. The army is to follow the leaders, just as the leaders follow the Lord; and there must be no contention among them. The Israelites with Joshua responded:

> *"All that you have commanded us we will do, and wherever you send us we will go. Just as we obeyed Moses in all things, so we will obey you. Only may the LORD your God be with you, as he was with Moses! Whoever rebels against your commandment and disobeys your words, whatever you command him, shall be put to death. Only be strong and courageous."* [7]

This is very serious business! Pondering it, I found a prophetic word delivered on May 19th, 2006:

> The army is ready to be sent in; army boots for every person, the army is coming in; they are ready, they are ready to go. Many have waited for this.

> I look to the East, West, North and South; release the warriors. Men of God rise up, rise up for it is time; you have been prepared. It is time; stand back no longer. Women, you must let the men come forward; it is time for your men to come forward. Release, release, release. I am cleansing the sins that have been defiled by ungodly women for generations back. You did not have the only responsibility to take the earth. Witchcraft has been

released on the land because of ungodly authority. Confession, confession, confession; I am a forgiving God, but the sins of the land you carry. The strategy of the enemy is to capture power. I have released this day godly power from deep within the earth, which has been held. That power must not get into the wrong hands; it must not be captured by ungodly women.

A nation is birthed; I have birthed a new thing. My glory will be released, My glory is coming forth. Do not stop My glory. Judgment; the sword is being released. Heed the words, time is short, you have been prepared, you have been trained. It's time to go out. Take no glory for your own; I will not share My glory. I will use those in who are in unity, in oneness, not preferring one to another. I will use the least of these; I will use the despised; do not judge with your eyes. It's springtime, a new springtime. The waters are muddy, but it will run off to be pure. The river is mine; it is pure from my throne. Judge not with your eyes.

The youth; I am bringing the young. Do not turn them aside this time. You must welcome them; you must embrace them; you must father them. I will show you My heart is in them.

Do not rationalize with your eyes. The people younger than twenty years will be the ones to enter into my glory. They are the ones who will see my power. They watch, standing off as you lead them in circles to the desert they didn't want to be in; they are weary and tired.

The youth that you think are the worst have the most power; they are the leaders. They can stand against the enemy because they can recognize the enemy and know its weaknesses. Like David living with the Philistines, they have lived with the enemy. They know the enemy's weaknesses.

I am trying to prepare you; do not reject what I am doing. The youth are hiding from you, but I am getting ready to bring them back. The time of those who tried to take their lives is coming to an end. This young generation will be the mighty army of God that comes into the Promised Land. Be careful. Be careful, be careful; do not despise them. See with my eyes what I see; hear with my ears; fulfill in your heart what I have put in you. Stop being religious; stop being self-righteous; just be my children, just walk with me. My glory will do the rest. I will begin to bring the youth to you. Love them; be the mother and father to them that they need. They will take you into the Promised Land. These are the ones who will show you how to cross the river; you cannot go in unless they go in with you. This is My word, and I never change.

This is Joshua's army.

I have waited sixteen years to see this come to pass, and it is now happening. Why are we doing meetings to encourage and train the youth? Why are we training leaders? First of all, because the Lord is sending us, but also because people need the Lord. During the Jesus Movement, Steven Green wrote the song, *People Need the Lord,*[8] which speaks of the emptiness of everyday life, fear, heartache and pain, all of which remains relevant today, and perhaps even more so.

I have about 2.5 million miles with American Airlines, and learned long ago that the fastest way to travel is to watch movies. I do not watch R-rated films so I am constantly looking for movies that are appropriate. Recently, as I was scrolling through the list of movies I saw one called *American Utopia*, which is also a Broadway play. The film is a reproduction of the actual musical, which was recorded live in a southern state. The musical starts with a ridiculous song that has difficult-to-understand lyrics. As the movie continued, I actually found myself not paying much attention to the words because the music itself is quite captivating. But as soon as I turned on the closed captioning function so I could understand, the reality of the nonsensical nature of the lyrics quickly became apparent.

The final song is performed with great excitement, but the words are nothing less than strange. The paraphrased message is, "We are on the road to nowhere, knowing what we want. Why don't you come along?" Nothing makes sense, and we are going nowhere, but don't worry, just be happy. Is this the purpose of our lives? What a sad, distorted view of the reality that is the marvelous life the Living God has given us.

So what is the purpose of our lives? I'm at the stage now where I could retire, but for what purpose? I don't because my life is for God's glory, for the King and His Kingdom. That is the best purpose; that is the greatest romance; it is also the greatest conflict and the greatest adventure. On my way to Hawaii on American Airlines again, I found another movie called *Dear Evan Hansen*, about a teenager who is unable to function in life, so he writes letters to himself. Eventually, a boy with whom he has a brief conversation, commits suicide. Evan meets with the boy's family, who is convinced he is a true friend; they are relieved to think that their loved one enjoyed a friendship. Though that is not true, Evan enters into the deception. The movie, also a Broadway play, is filled with songs that express desperation and hopelessness. It ends with no suggestion regarding the purpose of life, or why we are alive on the earth. No answer is ever given to the question, "What is the meaning of life?"

Why do we battle for the Lord? We battle so that people who cannot find any meaning in their lives can see the truth of the Gospel of Jesus Christ. We battle so that people will know our wonderful Lord and find true fulfillment in serving Him. We battle so that people can be saved and set free from all the evil that has plagued them and their families for generations. We battle so that people can enter into the freedom of the Lord and live a life of fulfillment, peace, and rest in the joy of the Lord. We battle because the Word of God provides the real answer to the reason why we are on this earth.

Life is not meaningless and nonsensical, but scripture is clear that a life apart from Jesus has no purpose. Without Him there is no one to find you, no one to rescue you. The battle is difficult; in fact, battling is exhausting, but what other choice do we have?.

For years I've done many sessions of personal ministry, becoming both physically and mentally exhausted from the battle. At the same time, Donna has often been in tremendous pain. I would go out to soak in my Jacuzzi at night, sit there and pray, "Lord, I don't know if I can keep doing this; I'm so tired and Donna is suffering. People I work with are in pain, we are all in pain, and this is very hard." Then I would remember a song by Bill and Gloria Gaither, and sing it in the Jacuzzi, *I Will Serve Thee.*[9] The song speaks of the reason Jesus died on Calvary, which was to give us life and save us from the heartaches and broken pieces of our lives. He is the reason I continue; He is the reason we persevere. I will serve Him because of I love Him; He has given life to me.

One day at Downey First Baptist Church in 1966, as the organist played the old hymn, *So Send I You* during the offertory, the Lord called me to ministry. The song's message is a call to serve the Lord in battle, clearly indicating that the price of service is high because one can expect to be unrewarded, ridiculed, unknown and even hated. Isaiah faced a similar call to offer his life for service to God:

> *And I heard the voice of the Lord saying, "Whom shall I send, and who will go for us?" Then I said, "Here I am! Send me." And he said, "Go, and say to this people: " 'Keep on hearing, but do not understand; keep on seeing, but do not perceive.' Make the heart of this people dull, and their ears heavy, and blind their eyes; lest they see with their eyes, and hear with their ears, and understand with their hearts, and turn and be healed."* [10]

Like Isaiah, I said, "Here I am, send me." Like Isaiah, many of my friends have also said, "Here I am, send me." For none of us has life been easy, because we are in the middle of a war, and it's not World War III. It's the war of the ages in which evil pulls out all the stops to cripple the advancement of the Kingdom of God on earth as it is in the heavens; it's the war between darkness and light, the Light of the World; it's a war that, apparently, the enemy still mistakenly thinks he can win. We are going into battle; we have crossed over, and we are going to fight. This is a commission from the Lord that can also be yours, should you choose to receive it. What will your answer be?

---

[1] Type — a figure, representation, or symbol of something to come, as an event in the Old Testament foreshadows another in the New Testament. Types generally find their fulfillment in the person and ministry of Christ, but they sometimes relate to God, His people, or some other reality.

Youngblood, R. F., Bruce, F. F& Harrison, R. K., Thomas Nelson Publishers, eds. (1995). In *Nelson's new illustrated Bible dictionary*. Thomas Nelson, Inc.

[2] *The Holy Bible: English Standard Version* (Wheaton, IL: Crossway Bibles, 2016), Jos 1:9.

[3] Ibid., Jos 1:2–3.

[4] Ibid., Joshua 1:7–8. .,

[5] Ibid., Joshua 1:11.

[6] Ibid., Joshua 1:13–15.

[7] Ibid., Joshua 1:16–18.

[8] Both the lyrics and a video of Steve Green performing are available at: https://zionlyrics.com/lyrics/steve-green-people-need-the-lord-lyrics

[9] Music with lyrics available at: https://www.youtube.com/watch?v=4o1Pq3U2QP0

[10] *The Holy Bible: English Standard Version* (Wheaton, IL: Crossway Bibles, 2016), Is 6:8–10.

CHAPTER NINE:
IT ALL COMES TOGETHER

Sometimes it is only in the writing of a book that many 'moving parts' suddenly come together to form a bigger picture. As has been clear throughout the *Exploring Heavenly Places* series, prophetic words from many years past, even those we thought we already understood, have become relevant again as the Lord reveals deeper and deeper levels of understanding. In researching this volume, it has astounded us how many of the words that speak of unity also include grace, sound and battle. In the words of *The A-Team's* Hannibal Smith, for those old enough to remember, "I love it when a plan comes together." Make no mistake, the plan over which we are rejoicing is God's!

While many prophetic words have been included thus far, here we'd like to share what we're calling 'crossover words', with concepts pertaining to **unity**, **grace**, **sound** and **battle**:

March 6, 2005: **Unity** is a spiritual concept; nothing can stop the people then if they are in complete **unity**. Look and see what happens when there is **unity**; **enemy attacks unity** with all force. Don't worry about satan, we are destroying the church by our disunity; we refuse to bite the bullet and work it out.

November 2005: (We're up so high I can see the tops of trees.) I'm synchronizing you; everything, the **vibration**, the **sound**, the light, the oil, the blood, the water. Tap in; tap in freely to all that God has; begin to just tap in to the glory, to the healing, to the anointing. The anointed ones are here; we just need to tap in. Administer it to others; share it; give it freely; bring others up high to the heart of Jesus, to bring the five-fold together in each person. New tabernacle coming through; we're the new offerings in the tabernacle, and the revelation can only come in the context of **unity**.

August 2007: I'm breaking the yokes off my people; you're no longer under the law, you're under my **grace**. It's a new time, a new era, and you are to live in my **grace**, in **unity**. I give you hope for a future that you haven't known, a future of love and peace and joy and **harmony** without bitterness or roots of bitterness… I am establishing a new time and a new era, and you are to walk in my **grace** and my love in unity. I am calling you to unite in my Spirit, my Oneness. It's the tree of **unity**, the tree of life.

August 2007: I make all things new; I make all things new. You're a new creation; I'm still creating; I'm still making one in the heavens, and if you can see one in the heavens it's on earth. You've tasted the good word, now taste of the age to come; it's not a new beginning but all things made new. You're on the other side, into a new **unity**, a new revision of **unity** that is a **sound** of thought in mind and deed.

2008: I'm bringing you **together** to make **one sound**. The enemy knows if we come **together**, we'll make the **sound** of the trumpet. The enemy tries to keep us apart. By yourself, you can do nothing. We're meant to be in **harmony** and **synchronized.** If any inanimate musical instruments, such as the flute or the harp, do not give distinct notes, how will anyone listening know or understand what is played? And if the **war bugle** gives an uncertain call, who will prepare for **battle?**"

November 2008; Babylon; the harlot is here; the harlot is here. There must be more **unity, unity, unity**; this is a **call** for **unity**. One heart, one mind, one spirit for the **war** is on. There is a **war. Warring** angels have been sent forth. Sent forth across the land, across the sea, across the ports.

November 2008: Feed my sheep, and also something about horses, something about this group and horses. It's about running with the swiftness, strength and might of a horse, and shaking the ground as you go, you'll **sound** like thunder when you go in **unity**. The **unity** of **sound** is linked with **battle**.

March 2009: Wheel within a wheel. Surround **sound**. Seven spirits burning. It's new height, new depth, new dimensions. You haven't been here yet. A new witness in the earth. The river is here. Your roots are connected. This you know is true, but now get ready to experience true **unity**. You are coming through to the new.

August 2009: **Unity, unity**; It's not what you think. You should support each other while you are standing on the brink. Breakthrough is coming, don't be caught short. Watch your **words**; they will crush or kill. They should bring life so the lame will be healed. Counsel is mine, sound wisdom is mine, and understanding as well. You are hand-picked for such a time as this.

October 17, 2009: The Lord is cutting walls between the people, cutting down walls of division. Look out and see My creation; see My stars that I have created. Hear their **voice**, hear their **sound**. You say, "Twinkle, twinkle little stars," but they are not little. They radiate my light; they **vibrate** with me. It is **one note, one chord, one vibration**: they **sing together one note**; it is the **sound** of My creation. I spoke and they were created. They **sing** in **unity**; they **sing** in **harmony**. They radiate my light. This is what I have called you to do; you can transverse My light, you can travel on My light beams in heavenly places. You can come up above the discord, the division. This is My purpose. Hear the **sounds**; I am tuning you even now to hear the **sound**. I am lining you up according to Me; I am changing your molecular structures, your elements, your building blocks; I am shifting them, realigning them.

May 2010: This is the new way, a living way. Test these stones, the living stones; they **vibrate**, they regenerate, they **sing**; they are built together in **unity**. There is a **sound** in the stones, and in **unity** it is released. They hold wealth and they hold increase. Remove the structure in common union, for your declaration is at hand. It is about your **words**; they are connected to the heart. As you think, so you are. There is something old and something new, but for now, pray and you will break through.

May 2010: You are creating a pathway, a true way for the Bride to cross over. Gather the revelation, the information that will be built upon for acceleration. Your perception will position you; you are growing wiser; you join in the light for your revelation. There's healing and deliverance in the streams of light. You **connect one to another**; it's for **unity** that you win this **fight**.

April 2013: Many sacrifices have been made by those in this room so others can come. You have chosen the foundations of the earth when you stood before the throne and counted the cost. You have walked away from friends, and family and finances; you have taken up your cross and not looked back. You are my sons, my beloved. You must continue the course in **unity** for there is great **warfare** against your **oneness**. There is **one mind** and **one purpose**—to radiate the Son of Man who is even now in your midst. For your heart is a **song** and your life is a **melody**. There are the minor keys; release the major keys. Army major, army major, for you release the hearts of **warriors** for the days to come. It's about **unity, unity of heart, unity of mind, unity of spirit**; it's a marriage. Your marriage is worship; your marriage is fragrant. Call many into marriage; call My people back to marriage, a marriage with My Son, be **one** with Him, **united** to Him. Be restored to him; restoration, restoration, restoration.

October 2013: There's fire, wind and rain in the clouds…and **sound**…My word comes forth in the clouds; My **voice** is heard through the clouds. They transmit My **voice** to be heard. It's the **sound** of thunder, the **sound** of thunder to cleanse. I'm releasing My **voice** in the cloud. The **audible voice** of the Lord is coming to you in the cloud; you will hear me louderrrrr, louderrrrr. Wake up and strengthen yourselves…**Gather together** amongst yourselves; there is strength in **unity**. strength in **unity**, strength in **unity**, strength in **unity**. I have designed you before the beginning of time to be in **unity**, **unified**. I've designed you to be unified from the beginning of time, to be **in community**. Strengthen yourselves in one another and in me. I give you strength for the **battle**, for every **battle**. I give you strength, strength for your bones. I'm calling you to greater things. I'm calling you to greater measures so strengthen yourselves. Get ready for the greater things. I'm **sounding the trumpet**! I'm **sounding the alarm**! Awake! Awake! Awake oh, sleeper; awaken to My presence within you, to My fire within you. I'm sending you out to release the glory that was established before the foundations of the earth and the time is now, not tomorrow.

February 2016: A **sound** of dissonance has shattered the lines of inheritance. A **unity** of disharmony a broken path, an electric magnetic field that pulls you to attract. But the highways of holiness aligned to the heart that **sound** of resonance is where you start. It's the path that you've trodden, which levels the place, and creates the path of righteousness; for Zion is your escape. A collective sea of transparency is where you stand, the order of Melchizedek is at His right hand. This collective sea has a **sound** of **unity** a fourfold return…the things that were shattered are restored in the heart.

November 2017: Open, open, open; every door has a way to **unity** for the glory so the power will display. On Earth as it is in Heaven, you hold the keys; unlock the age for power, and in the glory they all agree. Hope is a tangible certainty of **grace** so pour out the evidence of faith as the waters cover this place.

June 2018: It is important to know; to know me as the holy one is to be set apart for the glory of the Lord. I say this because of the paradigm in the past. Their ruling seeks to have a way that is connected to the law and not **grace**. The anointing has not yet been experienced to what it could be for it was always in you to break the yoke and set the captives free...I now speak to you about **unity**, which is the goal; not one without the other so the anointing will flow. Find **agreement** with me. Search out the matter to **unify** these parts and set them free. My plan is to prosper and bring great assurance. Any contradiction or conflict causes double mindedness. This is why I speak to the eyes of the heart, for when the heart is not fully convinced, the parts stay apart.

October 2018: There is a heart cry of **unity** that the Lord can hear; it joins with the Lion of Judah so the strong right arm of the Lord can heal. From the gates of thankfulness there is a connection to the original self; a deep, deep well of **unity** and the **sound** is in the water; the water stirs up and up to heal the parts. For the Lord is always listening; He always can see; He is always ready to assist when these parts believe.

January 2019: Strength is in **unity**; power flows through **unity**; love flows through **unity** and this is what I require of you, the love and the **unity**…Submit one to another, love your sister and your brother. You are **each a part of each other and a part of Me**. My kingdom working through you, working in **unity**. Things are heating up and it's time to move. It's 'blast off' time. I'm bringing you **together**, to make **one sound**. The enemy knows if we come **together**, we'll make the **sound** of the trumpet. The enemy tries to keep us apart. By yourself, you can do nothing.

March 2021, at an Aslan's Place Academy: The key to healing is us, operating in unity. (Paul discerned **unity**, along with waves and waves of power.) The power comes from the Lord, and in our **unity** there is a **unity gain**,[1] so the power is not affected by us and it flows out…(Paul feels healing, which is connected to **unity**)…**Unity** comes when we are consecrated. **Unity wars**; it is in our **unity** that we can **war** against evil.

September 2021: Time in and time out, time to expect that you're never without. Take back from the mighty ones and the ancients long ago; this is the platform of justice, to restore what was left behind in time from before. Bring it to the fullness of time, and righteousness that goes before will align. The glory of the Lord will be your rear guard. **Frequencies** will align the true **sound** of joy It is in the **unity** and the glory of the lord will be known.

September 2021: The Lion of Judah is **roaring** against His enemies…There is a strategic linking up of different ministries that will not necessarily be under one umbrella, but will be under the Son of God. A brotherhood, a sisterhood that minister together **unity**. It is about the **unity** of heart and purpose…It is time to move forward by faith and courage. Not all will understand, not all will come into **unity**. Not all will appreciate, but there will be a remnant **warrior army** that the Lord will draw and ministry shall be reproduce. It is the only way to bring down the enemy. You cannot hold back. There will be persecution, there will criticism, but you cannot hold back. This will take great courage, stamina and perseverance.

January 2022: On a piano when you hit one chord there are three notes. We are supposed to rise up with that **sound**. Without the chord, it is going to be broken. **Unity** is the key.

I (Barbara) can affirm the power of unity with sound. For several years, I sang barbershop with an award-winning Sweet Adelines chorus that regularly competed with other choruses. We were always striving to get every aspect of a tune exactly right—word perfect, note perfect, timing perfect—so that the blend of about 35 individual voices singing four different notes would come together in such harmony that the tones would literally send shivers down your spine. Every once in a while we would hit that perfect chord and produce a unique sound, an overtone or 'fifth voice', which could be clearly heard:

> The precise synchrony of the waveforms of the four voices simultaneously creates the perception of a 'fifth voice' while at the same time melding the four voices into a unified sound.[2]

Whenever this occurred, it would not be unusual for us to stand in silence when the song was finished, stunned by the beauty of the harmony, with tears of emotion flooding our eyes. I liken that fifth voice to the voice of the Lord, chiming in when we come together in unity to seek Him.

Sadly, that same chorus has come to represent the power of unrighteous unity to me. Several years after leaving, I was invited back to an anniversary celebration in which the chorus performed. By then, they had become regional champions, which qualified them to compete in the yearly international competition, where they placed second for a small-sized chorus. Their sound was amazing, and I was awestruck by the incredible harmony. But my wonder soon fizzled as they began to sing one of their obviously favorite show tunes, *Jezebel.* I could only cringe inside as I listened to these talented ladies sing of the praises of that evil woman. Suddenly, the beautiful had become the profane.

Does that ever happen in our churches? I think it does. The focus of our unity must always be to glorify God in all things. But the enemy really doesn't like that so he warps our perception; and one day we wake up and realize the joy is gone. Why? Because we've lost our focus and have become unified behind programs, performance and attendance records, all of which probably have little or nothing to do with what the Father is doing. In August 2009, the following word was received:

> Rejoice, rejoice, rejoice. Rejoice because you are **becoming one with Me** with one heart, one spirit, one mind, one goal. Are you ready to be **joined with Me**, with my heart? **Unity, unity of the spirit, unity of the mind, unity of the heart. Single focus, single focus, single focus.**

Biblical unity is never characterized by the deception and torment that are flaunted in the lyrics of *Jezebel*. Rather, it's always harmonious, characterized by love:

> *Live in harmony with one another. Do not be haughty, but associate with the lowly. Never be wise in your own sight.*[3]

> *And above all these put on love, which binds everything together in perfect harmony. And let the peace of Christ rule in your hearts, to which indeed you were called in one body. And be thankful.*[4]

Consider again the early Church as described throughout Acts. They operated by **grace**, in **unity**, and their **testimony (sound)** was heard far and wide. Their message was **opposed (warfare/battle)** to the point that many were martyred; yet they persevered and God's power was poured out in signs and wonders, and evangelism exploded throughout the known world.

---

[1] An amplifier adds gain, but the unity gain means that the unity is not affected

[2] https://en.wikipedia.org/wiki/Overtone

[3] Romans 12:16

[4] Colossians 3:14-15

CHAPTER TEN:
UNITY OF THE SPIRIT

The biblical aspects of unity, along with an abundance of prophetic words, have been clearly documented. The need for unity did not magically disappear when the early church died out, though the enemy might like us to think so because denominational squabbles and infighting within the Body of Christ have served him well. Let's consider a couple historic admonitions for unity, going first to John Donne, well known as both a poet and a clergyman; a man who understood the need for unity. It is from him that we received a popular idiom that expresses well the fact that we can't live in isolation from others:

> 'No man is an island' is an idiom taken from a 1642 sermon by the Dean of St Paul's Cathedral. The Dean happened to be John Donne, a clergyman who now, almost four hundred years later, is regarded as one of the greatest English poets…[but] the words 'No man is an island' were embedded in a deeply Christian sermon about how human beings are connected to each other, and how important that connection is for the wellbeing and survival of any individual.[1]

Fast forward a couple of centuries to comments from a sermon that C.H. Spurgeon delivered on January 1, 1865:

> We dare not commit the sin of quenching the Holy Spirit, even though it were with the view of promoting unity. But the unity of the Spirit never requires any sinful support; that is maintained not by suppressing truth, but by publishing it abroad.

> First, there is a unity of the Spirit of which the text speaks, which is worthy to be kept. You will observe it is not an *ecclesiastical unity*, it is not endeavouring to keep the unity of the denomination, the community, the diocese, the

parish—no, it is "endeavouring to keep the unity of the Spirit.

But what is this unity of the Spirit? I trust, dear brethren, that we know it by having it in possession; for it is most certain that we cannot *keep* the unity of the Spirit, if we have it not already. Let us ask ourselves the question, "Have we the unity of the Spirit?" None can have it but those who have the Spirit, and the Spirit dwells only in new-born believing souls. By virtue of his having the Spirit, the believer is in union with every other spiritual man, and this is the unity which he is to endeavour to keep. This unity of the Spirit is manifested in *love*. A husband and wife may be, through providence, cast hundreds of miles from one another, but there is a unity of spirit in them because their hearts are one. We, brethren, are divided many thousands of miles from the saints in Australia, America, and the South Sea, but loving as brethren, we feel the unity of the Spirit. I was never a member of a Church meeting in the backwoods of America; I never worshipped God with the Samoans, or with my brethren in New Zealand; but notwithstanding all this, I feel the unity of the Spirit in my soul with them, and everything which concerns their spiritual welfare is interesting to me.[2]

Powerful words that bear repeating, "But the unity of the Spirit never requires any sinful support; that is maintained not by suppressing truth, but by publishing it abroad." Well said!

We can also attest to the truth of the fact that we may be divided by many miles, yet remail in unity of the Spirit with other believers. Paul has often spoken of how Jana Green, our friend to whom this book is dedicated, would often call him up to ask what he was up to now. Their spiritual connection was so strong that he would cheerfully complain that he couldn't get away with anything. I (Barbara) often get on a call with a friend in Africa whom I've never even met in person, and yet there's an instant connection as if we've known one another forever. Additionally, most of us can tell stories about experiences when someone was 'just thinking about you' and they called at exactly the moment you needed encouragement. That's unity; that's the way the Spirit of our Living God operates!

---

[1] https://nosweatshakespeare.com/quotes/famous/no-man-is-an-island/

[2] C. H. Spurgeon, "True Unity Promoted," in *The Metropolitan Tabernacle Pulpit Sermons*, vol. 11 (London: Passmore & Alabaster, 1865), 1–4.

CHAPTER ELEVEN:
FROM BEGINNING TO END - UNITY

Pondering how to introduce this chapter, I (Barbara) hear:

> *In the beginning was the Word, and the Word was with God, and the Word was God. He was in the beginning with God. All things were made through him, and without him was not any thing made that was made. In him was life, and the life was the light of men. The light shines in the darkness, and the darkness has not overcome it.[1]*

What better way then, to wrap things up? In the beginning was God, with Father, Son and Holy Spirit in perfect unity; and, to the end of our lives our need for oneness with Him is abundantly clear. In Jesus' own words:

> *The glory that you have given me I have given to them, that they may be one even as we are one, I in them and you in me, that they may become perfectly one, so that the world may know that you sent me and loved them even as you loved me.[2]*

As we have seen, unity with God is necessary if we are to do only what the Father is doing; unity within ourselves is required for the entirety of body, soul and spirit to function as God intended; and unity with others, while not always easy to achieve, is essential for success within the Body of Christ. We also know that either ungodly unity or disunity within the Body is a plague on mankind, rooted way back in the Garden of Eden with the first sin. Since the corruption of our unity because of sin is a given, a generational prayer to restore unity seems appropriate:

> Father, I renounce and repent on behalf of myself and my generational line back to before the beginning of time for all instances of nurturing misunderstandings, offenses, unforgiveness, bitterness, strife, division, jealousy, envy, and every other sin of disunity.[3]

I repent for fostering disunity, allowing ourselves and others to fall into the traps and snares of the enemy. I repent for not guarding our fellowship, but entering into strife, envy, deception, dishonesty, violence, grumbling, gossip and slander.

I repent for all ungodly passivity that caused us to come into agreement with unjust accusations, ungodly perceptions, ungodly images, word curses and limitations, which have been sent against me or anything that belongs to me. Lord, please cancel this evil and disconnect me from all of it. I choose not to compare myself with others, but to look to You for my identity; I choose to come into agreement with Your perception of me.

I repent for all worship of, or covenants with, foreign gods, idols and other ungodly beings.

Lord, in your mercy, please break off all evil that has opened any doors that would allow division in my life. Also, please close all ungodly doors of disunity, and open the righteous doors of unity so the gates cannot be shut against me.

I declare Your truth, *Blessed be the Lord, who has not given us as prey to their teeth! We have escaped like a bird from the snare of the fowlers; the snare is broken, and we have escaped!* [4] I declare that the enemy will now fall victim to the traps and snares set against me.[5]

Lord, please release your blessings to me, and to all relationships in my life and family line.

Earlier, Paul wrote:

Like Isaiah, I said, "Here I am, send me." Like Isaiah, many of my friends have also said, "Here I am, send me." For none of us has life been easy, because we are in the middle of a war, and it's not World War III. It's the war of the ages in which evil pulls out all the stops to cripple the advancement of the Kingdom of God on earth as it is in the heavens… This is a commission from the Lord that can also be yours, should you choose to receive it. What will your answer be?

Those in the early Church were warriors, and if we are truly soldiers of the Cross we should be as willing as they were to engage in the battle; for the final harvest is quickly approaching:

Jesus said to them, "My food is to do the will of him who sent me and to accomplish his work. Do you not say, 'There are yet four months, then comes the harvest'? Look, I tell you, lift up your eyes, and see that the fields are white for harvest.[6]

I do not ask for these only, but also for those who will believe in me through their word, that they may all be one, just as you, Father, are in me, and I in you, that they also may be in us, so that the world may believe that you have sent me. The glory that you have given me I have given to them, that they may be one even as we are one, I in them and you in me, that they may become perfectly one, so that the world may know that you sent me and loved them even as you loved me. Father, I desire that they also, whom you have given me, may be with me where I am, to see my glory that you have given me because you loved me before the foundation of the world. O righteous Father, even though the world does not know you, I know you, and these know that you have sent me. I made known to them your name, and I will continue to make it known, that the love with which you have loved me may be in them, and I in them.[7]

So, once again, the question is, "What will your answer be? Will you join the battle and cry, "Here I am, send me?"

---

[1] John 1:1-5

[2] John 17:22-23

[3] Proverbs 26:20-21; 1 Corinthians 3:3; Proverbs 6: 16-19, 26:20-21; 1 Timothy 5:13, Proverbs 11:13, John 6:41-42; Romans 1:29-32

[4] Psalm 124:6-7

[5] Psalm 141:10

[6] John 4:34-35

[7] John 17:20-26

CONCLUSION

Throughout this book, the Lord has woven together a tapestry of unity; but when we first began we had only four chapters with no idea how He was going to weave grace, sound, and the battle into a bigger picture that would fill the pages. So began the search into prophetic words, and soon it became clear that unity was the underlying theme that connected it all.

Fanny J Crosby, sometimes called the 'Queen of Gospel Song Writers', penned the words of *To God be the Glory* around 1872. It was then introduced during D.L. Moody's evangelistic campaigns during 1873-1874. Later, it was popularized by Cliff Barrows at Billy Graham crusades in the 1950s, soon making its way it into most modern hymnals.[1] An 'oldie but goodie', it expresses well our gratitude to the Lord for the way He crafted this book:

> To God be the glory, great things He hath done;
> So loved He the world that He gave us His Son,
> Who yielded His life an atonement for sin,
> And opened the life gate that all may go in.
>
> Praise the Lord, praise the Lord,
> Let the earth hear His voice!
> Praise the Lord, praise the Lord,
> Let the people rejoice!
> O come to the Father, through Jesus the Son,
> And give Him the glory, great things He hath done.

---

[1] https://en.wikipedia.org/wiki/To_God_Be_the_Glory

APPENDIX ONE

PRAYER TO RELEASE THE JOYFUL SOUND

I renounce and repent on behalf of myself and my family line back to before the beginning of time for:

- Listening to and aligning with ungodly sounds
- Coming into agreement with dissonance and disunity in any way
- Buying into or accepting the enemy's corrupted version of the seven Spirits of God or the seven Eyes of the Lord
- Honoring God with lips while our hearts were far from Him
- Any participation in ungodly worship through music, rhythms or dance
- Listening to ungodly worship
- All use of music as part of ungodly sacrifices

Father, Son and Holy Spirit I acknowledge that you are the Master Conductor and that You determine the time signature of the sound movements of my life, and the composition of the notes of my life. Lord please:

- Remove any contamination off the righteous seven eyes as they manifest through my life so that the sound of the Lord may go through the ends of the earth
- Recover my birthright of righteous light sound that has been stolen and trapped in ungodly stars, false sounds, frequencies and cycles
- Retune, realign, and/or replace the sounds and vibrations of any of the three chords connected to parts of my body, mind, and soul which are out of tune

- Remove all ungodly 'star sounds' in my body, soul and spirit, and correct all ungodly dissonance so that my body, soul and spirit now emits the correct sounds that are to the Praise of Your Glory
- Release palmoni[1] to set the correct vibrations in my body, soul and spirit back to Your original created design
- Cause my living stones to vibrate to your original created design, and restore Your proper chord structures in my life and family line
- Break all ungodly ties between me and ungodly beings that were established in any way including through ungodly worship
- Replace ungodly beats and rhythms with Your heartbeat
- Align my God given song to the symphony of Your body so that we are of one accord.[2]
- Release into me the correction of sound that took place at the Cross
- Release into me the sound of every word Jesus spoke on earth
- Remove all ungodly powers that have encapsulated every musical star chord

APPENDIX TWO

The Power of Homothumodon in the Early Church
(Reference, Acts 1-8, 12-15 & 18 KJV or NKJV)

Homothumodon (being of one accord, locking arms with the same purpose)	Fruit/Blessings of Homothumodon	Demonic Response to the Church being in one accord
Prayer in one accord in the upper room	The outpouring of the Holy Spirit on the Day of Pentecost	Mockery
The Spirit empowers the 120 disciples as they wait in one accord for the promise of the Spirit	3,000 Jews receive Jesus as the Messiah	None
The church in Jerusalem meets in one accord in the temple courts and I one another's homes	The Lord adds to their number daily as they meet one another's needs; A man lame from birth is healed and the number of men in the Church grows to 5,000	Intimidation
After Peter & John are released, they go back to their people and pray in one accord for boldness to continue sharing the gospel message in Jerusalem with signs and wonders	The disciples, filled with the Spirit, begin to speak boldly about Jesus in the face of strong persecution They share their possessions with one	None

following	another, and with great power continue to testify to the resurrection while performing signs and wonders	
The believers meet in one accord at Solomon's Colonnade in the temple	More people are added to the number of believers and begin to speak boldly about Jesus	Jealousy
Members of the Synagogue of Freedmen falsely accuse Stephen in one accord and bring him before the Sanhedrin for questioning, culminating in him being stoned in one accord	Stephen, full of grace and power, performs great wonders and miraculous signs among the people	Sorcery, as Simon, a magician is saved; but then out of ignorance tries to purchase the power of God for his own means, with other accounts of sorcery as Acts continues
Philip, one of those scattered through-out Judea and Samaria goes into a city and proclaims Jesus, with miraculous signs following as the people listen in one accord to his message	This was the first non-Jewish city reached for Christ	None
An angel of the Lord frees Peter from prison after the Church prays in one accord	When King Herod realizes Peter has escaped, leaves Judea for Caesarea	None

Paul, Barnabas, the apostles of Jerusalem and the Church elders meet to discuss if Gentiles must convert to Judaism, with the matter finally being resolved in one accord; a decree is issued and a letter is sent to notify the Gentile churches	The Gentile churches of Antioch, Syria and Cilicia are encouraged that they don't have to become Jews before becoming Christians	None
None	None	When Gallio is proconsul of Achaia, there is a united in-one-accord attack on Paul to drag him into court
When writing to the church in Rome, Paul addresses the issue of passing judgment on disputable matters, encouraging the believers to make every effort to build one another up; later he prays for God to give them the spirit of unity so that with one heart and mind (one accord) they may bring glory to God	None	None